"In the tsunami of media and messages chasing us from our smartphones, laptops, and televisions, it's easy to give up the notion that our own voice can ever be heard—or even matters. Denise is a brilliant marketer and brand strategist, and her book shows us not only how to stand out in a crowd, but how to tower above it. Like its author, Forty Dollars and a Brand is intelligent, accessible, fun, unpredictable, high impact, and global."

- Ron Stodghill,
award-winning business journalist and author

"*Forty Dollars and a Brand* does add up to awesomeness. This is a good investment, in my book."

- Jack Agnew,
senior counsel, MSL Group

"The personal triumphs and professional accomplishments of my longtime and dear friend, Denise Kaigler, are well known and greatly admired. In Forty Dollars and a Brand, Denise has applied her mantra of self-examination, hard work, optimism, and professionalism into winning combinations. This book is a perfect vehicle for self-improvement and potential realization."

- Fletcher "Flash" Wiley,
Boston attorney, businessman, and essayist

"Forty Dollars and a Brand is an intensely personal account of what can happen when one looks in the mirror and sees who she has the potential to be and the impact she has the power to make on others. A must-read for those who are serious about learning how to communicate who they are, what they do, and why it should matter to others."

- Tenley-Ann Hawkins,
public relations consultant

"Denise Kaigler lays her soul bare as she reveals the complexities of discovering her personal brand. Forty Dollars and a Brand is deeply inspirational and a top pick for those who aspire to develop and market their personal brand in ways that help them reach their goals and live their dreams."

- Bryony Bouyer,
senior vice president, Hasbro

PRAISE FOR DENISE KAIGLER AND MDK BRAND MANAGEMENT, LLC

"Denise's personal branding workshop was thought provoking and empowering. It cautioned me that if I don't define myself, someone else can and will. This workshop helped me position myself in a unique way so that I stand out from others, enabling me to pursue my passions with confidence."

- Jehana Ray,
branding head, Fresenius Medical Care Renal Home Therapies
(formerly with Boston Scientific)

"I admired the skill with which Denise ran her personal branding workshop. For a dozen years, I was an associate director of the Derek Bok Center for Teaching and Learning at Harvard, where my enjoyable duties included running workshops for new teachers of Harvard undergraduates. I know how hard it can be to elicit participation from volunteers, and to draw out observations from them and the rest of the group. Denise did this extremely well. It was a pleasure to watch!"

- Richard F. Olivo, PhD,
Smith College

"As our seniors prepare to enter the workforce, understanding how to develop and nurture their personal brand is an extremely valuable skill to add to their professional toolbox. Denise delivers an understanding of the importance of personal branding, then proceeds to deliver the "know-how." I am pleased to have MDK Brand Management as a partner in student athlete personal development."

- Charlie Titus,
vice chancellor, University of Massachusetts Boston

"Early in your professional career, people will remind you that presentation matters, and that you only have a few seconds to make a first and lasting impression. That sage advice is true for a corporation or an individual, and is transferable no matter the age. Denise and MDK Brand Management provided our group of young professionals with a clear roadmap to personal branding that will pay dividends throughout their careers."

- Michael Curry, Esq.,
board member, National NAACP,
past president, NAACP Boston

"Denise effectively used her personal branding challenges as she climbed the corporate ladder to develop and facilitate relevant and engaging brand management workshops and strategic initiatives. Denise's tips on developing a strong and empowered personal brand are on point and have been well received by individuals who have attended her sessions. Everyone can benefit from her guidance!"

- Allyce Najimy, CEO,
The Foundation To Be Named Later

"Denise did a wonderful job engaging our youth at the Ron Burton Training Village. She took 120 teenagers through a five-week hour-long training session. She helped our young men understand the importance of developing and protecting their personal brand through a series of interactive and challenging exercises. Denise is easy to work with, a true professional, and brings great energy to her training sessions."

- Phil Burton,
Ron Burton Training Village

FORTY DOLLARS
AND A BRAND

Enjoy the journey!

Denni

FORTY DOLLARS AND A BRAND

How to Overcome Challenges, Defy the Odds and Live Your Awesomeness

DENISE KAIGLER

Brand Strategist and Founder of MDK Brand Management, LLC

MILL CITY PRESS - MAITLAND

Mill City Press, Inc.
2301 Lucien Way #415
Maitland, FL 32751
407.339.4217
www.millcitypress.net

Printed in the United States of America

ISBN-13: 978-1-63505-474-3

Dani and Joey, you are the rhythmic beats of my heart. I love you.

Family first: Joey, Denise, and Danielle in Providence, RI

This book is dedicated to individuals who are striving to strengthen their self-confidence and overcome challenges. Believe you can, and you will.

Disclaimer:

To protect the identities of some of my former colleagues referenced in this book, an alias is used instead of their real name.

CONTENTS

FORTY DOLLARS AND A BRAND

It was the summer of 1984 and I was a twenty-one-year-old college student living alone in a studio apartment in Boston's South End. One day I woke up hot, scared, and hungry. It had been two weeks since I'd received a paycheck from one of my part-time jobs. A search of my fridge and cabinets turned up a canister of flour, onions, and a bottle of cooking oil.

As a struggling and resourceful independent student, I cut up the onions, dipped the slices in flour, and fried them. Onion rings for breakfast, lunch, and dinner. The next day, I felt ill. I hadn't eaten a meal in two days. And I didn't expect any money for another week. Fear engulfed me. How was I going to survive the next seven days with no food and no one to ask for help?

A friend called. She heard the sound of my voice and asked if I was okay. I explained that, no, I was not. I didn't have any food or money. I had no idea what I was going to do. My friend, who was in no position to offer any financial assistance, expressed her concern and said she would check on me again soon.

A couple of hours later, my apartment buzzer sounded. It was Sammy, my friend's uncle. I hit the button to let him in. Sammy entered my apartment and told me that he had just received a call from his niece about my situation. He handed $40 to me and offered to take me to the grocery store. I began to cry. I hugged Sammy like my life depended on it. In a sense, it did. Sammy was making an investment in me and in my future. That $40 gift strengthened my resolve to overcome challenges and reinforced my desire to defy the odds and fulfill my dreams. Although I didn't realize it at the time, that heartening experience began to form the person, the brand, I would become: Dependable, driven, and compassionate.

***

Sisters Always: Debbie, Denise, and Dee Anne

Growing up in S.E., Washington, DC with my single mother, Diane, and two sisters, Dee Anne and Debbie, I spent my childhood believing it was normal to go from one challenging experience to the next. Day-to-day life was mostly about survival. My mother kept my sisters and me under her strict thumb and in constant fear of her thick pleather belt. My father, Michael, who was a college student when I was conceived and never married my slightly older mother, was an unwilling and absent parent. But that didn't stop me from worshipping the notion of him. For years I kept taped to my bedroom wall an old, yellowing newspaper clipping announcing his drafting by Vince Lombardi's famed Green Bay Packers. Unfortunately, my father's NFL career was as short-lived as his relationship with my mother.

As I transitioned to puberty, random violence became an increasing factor in my family's life. I was eleven years old when Ma was at work one day, and my sisters and I opened our apartment door to let in a friend. In an instant, a second girl burst in and the two much larger girls began beating up Dee, Debbie, and me, leaving us bloodied and bruised. When Ma came home and looked at us, she began to cry. I saw so clearly the weight she carried every day, fearing for the safety of her daughters while struggling to keep us fed, clothed, and sheltered. And it was in that very shelter that we had invited harm. It was a long time before I was able to wash away the shame of causing my mother so much pain.

BRUISED BUT NOT BROKEN

As a kid, I was awkward looking. I was tall and lanky and wore granny glasses. As if those pointy glasses weren't enough, at one point, I was forced to wear a patch over my right eye to strengthen my lazy left eye. It was horrible. My skin was pimple prone and my teeth were completely messed up. My mother couldn't afford to get braces for me, so I went through my adolescent years not smiling and lowering my head when I spoke. Every day, I would go in our apartment bathroom and smear Vaseline on the mirror, just at the point where my mouth appeared in the reflection. I would spend hours in that bathroom, talking to myself, smiling profusely, hoping against hope that my Vaseline-altered reflection would follow me out the door, down the street, and throughout life.

My three years at Hart Middle School in S.E. taught me more about street survival than algebra, chemistry, and creative writing combined could ever teach me about professional life. Nearly every day, I dutifully placed the fifty-cent stipend from Ma for recess snack-truck goodies in the claws of neighborhood thugs. It was a small price to pay for the right to go back to class with a full set of teeth. I never understood why there were no adult chaperones to protect us from senseless robberies in broad daylight.

I got teased a lot in school: "Hey, four-eyes," and "Where you going, buckteeth?" I was a painfully shy introvert, which made speaking up and defending myself an impossible reaction. My shyness was so bad that I was sometimes moved to tears of terror when a teacher called on me to answer questions in class.

In 1977, just as I was finishing ninth grade, Ma came home from work and announced that we were moving to Boston, Massachusetts. Ma, who didn't graduate from college, worked for NASA as an assistant assigned to special projects and was based at its Greenbelt, Maryland, office. We would live for one year in Boston where Ma would be a fellow at MIT (Massachusetts Institute of Technology) and Harvard University, studying computer programming and mathematics. I didn't understand it then, but seeing my mother overcoming obstacles, defying odds, and making possible the impossible made an indelible mark on me. That day etched in my mind's eye a picture of perseverance, strength, and confidence that would begin to shape a personal brand that would project those same qualities.

Although our move to Boston that summer went smoothly, despite my older sister Dee deciding to stay behind, I struggled with having no friends. I was still an introvert and felt more comfortable alone or with my younger sister, Debbie. I worried that having absolutely no other kids to eat lunch with or talk to at Brighton High School would become a mental and emotional hardship. I soon learned that wasn't to be the case. On my first day, I met my first love, fellow tenth-grader Cleve. He was 6'3" and the most handsome boy I'd ever met. For the next ten months, we were inseparable.

***

Seven years later (Cleve and I had broken up by then but remained close friends) I was able to graduate with a BA in broadcast journalism from Emerson College in Boston. Since I was an independent student responsible for funding my education, reaching that goal would not have been possible without part-time jobs, Pell grants, scholarships, student loans, and the support of a few special friends. Just a few months after graduating in 1985, I entered the professional world and the journey to discovering and living my awesomeness was underway. I began as a television news reporter, then became a public relations, corporate communications, marketing, and corporate branding leader, and am now an entrepreneur and adjunct professor.

Forty Dollars and a Brand: How to Overcome Challenges, Defy the Odds and Live Your Awesomeness is designed to help anyone who feels hindered by shyness, economic challenges, or other obstacles discover their self-confidence, believe in their potential, and fulfill their personal or professional goals. Throughout this book I share stories of my personal brand journey and the lessons I learned along the way. Also incorporated is a workbook of activities designed to guide the evolution of your brand as you march toward your awesomeness.

If I can, you can!

—Denise Kaigler

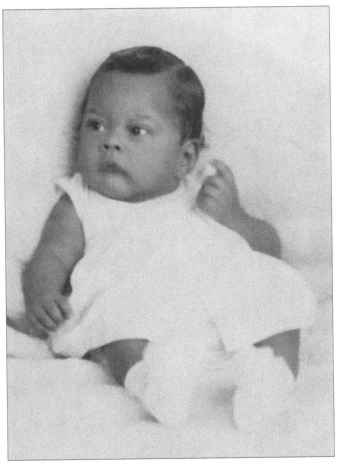

And so the adventure begins: Denise at three-months-old

PART 1

CREATING YOUR PERSONAL BRAND

CHAPTER 1

WHAT IS A PERSONAL BRAND?

"Your personal brand is your promise of value to the world, and your commitment to deliver distinctively with every skill developed and talents you have been gifted with."

—Bernard Kelvin Clive, personal branding coach

A personal brand is the way in which someone knows, understands, or could easily describe you. When you think of Oprah Winfrey, what words come to mind? When you see Barack Obama, Hillary Clinton, or Donald Trump, what emotions do you feel? When you hear the name Kim Kardashian or Justin Bieber, what's your immediate reaction? Each of these individuals has a well-known personal brand or, in other words, a distinct image or reputation. Whether you like them, dislike them, or are indifferent to them, you most likely know who they are and, more importantly, the personal traits that set them apart from the rest of us. They have transformed their brands into money-making machines.

While it may seem that some of the world's most visible personal brands were created overnight, many are the result of a meticulously crafted and marketed plan. As has been reported, Justin Bieber performed in shopping malls and parking lots, fine-tuning his musical skills and crafting his brand before hitting it big on the world stage. It's no secret that reality maestro Kris Jenner is credited with masterfully directing the Kardashian family from brand obscurity to obscene brand fame and wealth. Oprah Winfrey lived in poverty before her relentless message of optimism, self-improvement, and self-confidence helped catapult her brand worth to more than $3 billion as of June 2016, according to *Forbes*.

Confidence is an important element of personal branding. There were many moments in my career when my confidence was lacking. However, there was one notable moment when I had no choice but to display a level of confidence that was as distant from my inner being as Pluto is from Earth. It was the summer of 2002. NBA superstar and Reebok endorser Allen Iverson, widely regarded as an NBA bad boy, was arrested on several counts. Within minutes of Allen's court appearance being broadcast, Reebok's stock began to plummet. Several months earlier, Reebok signed a lifetime agreement with Allen and reinforced confidence in the sales of his signature footwear franchise, The Answer. As head of global public relations, I was in the hot seat. During an emergency meeting with Reebok chairman and chief executive Paul Fireman and members of his executive leadership team, I was told outright to do something to stop Reebok's stock from falling!

Wait. What? How am I supposed to do that?

Help was not flowing in my direction. I ran back to my office and gazed at my computer, hoping the answers to questions surrounding The Answer would magically appear. Not only was Allen's brand at stake, but the Reebok brand and my own personal brand were now on life support. My proposed strategy was to issue a short but very strong statement in support of Allen—no confusing words, no wavering, no room for anyone to read between the lines. I presented the strategy to Paul and the team. We needed to instill confidence in the broad community of Allen's supporters that Reebok wasn't about to leave Allen out on a limb to fend for himself, to find his own answers, and that we (Reebok and Allen) would survive the storm.

I presented the proposal to Paul. He gave me his approval to proceed. My personal brand was facing the most critical test of my career. Shortly after the Reebok statement was issued, my phone began ringing off the hook. One by one, I took the calls and repeated what reporters were reading while on the phone with me. And one by one, the stories with my quote were being published by media outlets, including *USA Today*:

USA Today excerpt, July 12, 2002:

Iverson's Reebok deal, which pays him an estimated $10 million annually and the bulk of his off-court earnings, comes via a "lifetime contract" he got just three years after being convicted of three felonies at age 18. Ad deals include so-called morals clauses allowing advertisers to escape ties with celebrities whose images become bad for business. But Thursday, Reebok spokeswoman Denise Kaigler didn't see a problem: "It's Allen's celebrity status, not facts, that continue to fuel these proceedings. We firmly believe Allen will be vindicated, and Reebok will be standing by him when he is."

Shortly after the Reebok statement made the rounds and the investment community realized that Reebok wasn't going to abandon Allen, our stock began to stabilize and then slowly climb. The relief running through my veins was palpable. On July 29, most of the charges against Allen were dropped. Allen's brand as a 'bad boy' would continue to excite and anger fans and foes alike, but, importantly, it was not going to lead to the demise of the Reebok brand or of mine. In fact, just a few years later, I was named Reebok's first senior vice president and chief communications officer and the first African American woman on Reebok's executive leadership team reporting directly to chairman and CEO Paul Fireman.

Though they may not be household names or millionaires, millions of people around the world also have a personal brand. These are individuals who are popular and highly respected or sought after for their particular expertise, opinions, or perspectives on various topics or issues. Perhaps you're someone who has something important to say, write, do or express but you're not established, popular, or sought after. Yes, even you, assuming you're over the age of, say, sixteen, have a personal brand. The key is to define, project, and protect that brand in ways that help you achieve your personal or professional goals.

Many years ago, following the completion of one of my work projects, a colleague said to me, "Denise, do you know what your brand is?" I gazed at him curiously. He quickly answered his own question: "You get sh*t done!" Hearing those words confirmed a reputation I'd been working hard to define and develop. My desired brand was to be known as someone who delivers results, gets the job done, hits the ball out of the park. During the past many years, I have enthusiastically fed my brand with experiences, activities, and behaviors that help to continuously strengthen, market, and project my brand of getting sh*t done and delivering results.

In addition to defining and projecting their personal brand, some of my clients are advised to protect their brand by using an often overlooked asset: A signature URL. Even if you never use it, securing your signature URL will ensure no one else can. Although there may be an annual hosting fee, this is an invaluable protection of your name from trolls who may offer to sell your URL to you for a hefty price or, worse, post inaccurate or harmful information on a site that appears to be sanctioned or owned by you.

Another undervalued and often misused asset when building your personal brand is the profile picture. I cannot tell you how many profile pictures I see that resemble mug shots! Would you go out with or hire someone who looks like they just rolled out of bed? Profile pictures posted on LinkedIn, Facebook, and other social networking platforms are so very important. Just as with online dating sites, profile pictures on professional or career sites also play a critical role in defining and marketing your personal brand. It is important to remember that your friends and family aren't the only people checking you out on those sites. Potential employers and employees, board members, community partners, college admission officers, investors, and loan officers may also be taking a stroll through your virtual world. Take the time and make the effort to put your best foot - and face - forward, both online and off.

Regardless of your background, status, or goal, strategizing a grand plan to build your brand can be a critical factor in helping you reach your personal goals or achieving your professional objectives. A strong and definitive personal brand can help you stand out from the crowd and project the confidence, focus, and drive that others want to connect with, be around, or even hire.

As you begin to build your Grand Brand Plan, take a selfie or have someone take a photo of you. It's a good idea to have 'before' and 'after' photographs to capture your physical brand evolution, assuming that a change in your appearance (e.g., clothes, hair, makeup, accessories) is part of the plan. Next, consider following the below chronological process, which you'll read about in more detail later:

a. **Open your mind:** No one is perfect. Be willing to do better and be better, to want more and be more, beginning with your brand.

b. **Identify your "why":** The process of building your brand begins with understanding not *what* you do, but *why* you do it. What you do will change throughout your life, but why you do what you do—why you are—is at the core of *who* you are. That will never change.

c. **Define your desired brand:** Decide what you want to be known for. Amazon founder Jeff Bezos said that "a personal brand is what people say about you when you're not in the room." What do you want people to say about you? I am sometimes asked whether it is best to have two different brands—one for work and one for home. I advise clients to define a brand that transcends their personal and professional worlds.

d. **Conduct a brand survey:** Don't just listen to the story you're telling yourself inside your head. Find out what stories others are telling about you.

e. **Write your elevator pitch:** How are you introducing yourself in a way that makes a strong impact and leaves a memorable impression?

f. **Find role models:** Surround yourself with people who project the brand you admire, respect, and want. Spend time with them. Attend networking events and professional conferences with them. Watch their interactions with others. See the impact they make.

g. **Establish your desired brand:** Take on the opportunities, exhibit the actions, and accept the projects that notably demonstrate with passion the bold and confident brand you want others to talk about in front of you *and* behind your back.

h. **Manage and maintain your desired brand**: Creating and distributing your personal business card, registering your signature URL and leveraging social media to establish your subject-matter expertise can help you maintain and manage your personal brand.

In the Part II Workbook, you will find this process outlined in six easy-to-follow steps that will help guide your path to defining, developing, and marketing your desired personal brand and living your awesomeness.

CHAPTER 2

WHY PERSONAL BRANDING MATTERS

A MATTER OF FACT

With more people going for the job you badly need or the promotion you desperately want, it is no longer enough to simply be. You must be seen. Being seen doesn't just happen. You make it happen. How you make it happen is critical.

In 2015, I founded my company, MDK Brand Management, LLC. Among my services, I develop brand building strategic initiatives as well as create and facilitate customized personal branding workshops. During my workshops, I regularly reference inspiring quotes or relevant articles from news outlets. One outlet that accurately and simplistically summarizes the impact of having a personal brand is *Fast Company*:

> It's something of a no-brainer, but there is a clear correlation between success and branding. Creating a strong brand establishes yourself as a natural leader, making people look up to you as a firm thought leader. The boost in image and direction opens doors and creates unique opportunities that would otherwise remain in the dark. Leadership qualities naturally evolve as success and branding interact with one another, which can launch a career into exciting new directions.

There is no question in my mind that having a well-defined and visible personal brand can positively impact your professional upward mobility. In 2000, while I was at Reebok, I was denied a promotion from senior director to vice president. The disappointing news hit me like a ton of bricks. I had all but bought that bottle of celebratory Dom Perignon. I remember looking at my boss and asking for the reason, something that I could wrap my head around and digest. His very direct answer floored me. He first explained that it wasn't his decision and that the CEO was personally approving or denying all requests for promotions to vice president and above. He then looked at me and offered this sage advice: Be seen!

Apparently, I wasn't in the face of the CEO enough. The CEO wasn't aware of my contributions to the strong results he was seeing and hearing about. I thanked my boss for his advice, then stood and walked out of his office, already strategizing in my head my next move. I knew that I first had to be willing to change myself in order to change the decision. This would no longer be status quo.

For the next many months, I focused on increasing my visibility and, in turn, elevating my brand. This wasn't about working harder. It was about working smarter. I began authoring summary reports following the completion of events, stepping out of my comfort zone by speaking up in meetings when I had constructive input, and taking the lead on major projects that involved or were of interest to the CEO. One such event was the press conference in December 2000 in New York to announce Reebok's historic contract with tennis star Venus Williams. Reebok never publicly confirmed the value of that contract so for the purpose of this book, I will only reference the media reports that estimated the agreement to be worth $40 million, reportedly making Venus the highest-paid female athlete ever. It was one of the most visible events Reebok had ever organized.

At the time, I was the company's senior director of global communications and oversaw the planning of the press event. Following the event, I created a comprehensive report detailing the media coverage and impressions. I wrote a cover note and hand-delivered the report to Reebok's key leadership. In July of 2001, during the next round of Reebok promotions, my elevation from senior director to vice president was approved. It was the first time I really understood the correlation between a well-defined and visible personal brand and upward progression.

In 2014 and 2015, while working full time in corporate, I volunteered my time facilitating personal branding workshops, just to see if there might be a market for a company that focused solely on brand management. It was rewarding to receive calls, e-mails, and notes from workshop attendees updating me on their careers and the impact of my branding advice. One note in particular had special meaning. It was from a young African American woman who attended one of my branding workshops for the NAACP Young Professionals Network members. She expressed her gratitude, telling me that the tips she learned during my workshop played a major role in the promotion she received at her company. Reading that note brought tears to my eyes.

THE WHYS HAVE IT

Defining who you are, what you are, and—maybe most importantly—*why* you are is an investment none of us can afford *not* to make. The United States Census reports that as of August 21, 2016, the world population reached 7.4 billion. The United States, the world's third most populous country, hit just under 325 million and is growing by one person every eleven seconds. If you're in your twenties, you're in good or bad company, depending on how you look at it. As of 2015, most of the US population shared your birth decade. California, Texas, Florida, New York, and Illinois—states with some of the most desirable metropolitan areas—round out the top five most populous states. These statistics paint the picture of the growing competition we're facing, and why projecting our unique set of brand attributes is increasingly important.

In 2014, best-selling author Simon Sinek urged his Ted Talk audience to "start with why." During his research, Sinek discovered that "not only did most companies fail to mention why they do what they do, but many of them don't even know why they do what they do."

By Sinek's thinking, it's no longer enough to differentiate your business by highlighting what your business does—you must define why your business does it. "People don't buy what you do. They buy why you do it," says Sinek.

Sinek helps illustrate the significance of "Why" in his infamous three-layer business marketing concept called "The Golden Circle."

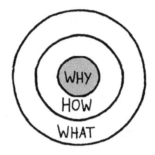

Although Sinek's Golden Circle focuses on business marketing, I believe it is just as relevant and critical to personal branding.

- "Why" do you do what you do?
- "How" do you do it?
- "What" do you do?

Remember those billions of people around the world, the hundreds of millions in the US, and the large number who are working professionals? Their presence means our "what" is no longer enough to stand out. It is our "why" that sets us apart. Why do you do what you do? Why should people care? When you interview for that job or go for that promotion, it is your "why" that will differentiate you from the competition or make you memorable to the hiring manager. When you are speaking at a conference or on a panel, your "why" may make your story more compelling and lead to additional speaking opportunities. So, that begs the question: What's the "why" of your personal brand? Take a look at the following list and see if any points resonate with you.

WHAT'S YOUR WHY?

- Your challenging childhood or upbringing
- Your prior lack of self-confidence and desire to help others like you
- Your past encounters with gender/race/pay equity issues
- Your perceived shortcomings or personal flaws
- Your difficult family relationships
- Your idyllic and balanced life and desire to now give back, mentor, or support

Given the sensitive topics of many of the examples listed, how and when to use your "why" will be critical. Consider your audience or goal before deciding to talk about your personal flaws or challenging childhood. Just as critical is making sure there is reasoning behind expressing your "why." Will disclosing your difficult family relationship while highlighting your professional strengths and accomplishments help set you apart from other candidates seeking your dream job of managing a youth crisis center? In addition to your potential boss recognizing your strengths, will he or she also view you as being more relatable to the center's target audience?

Your "why" is only part of your compelling brand story, it shouldn't be *the* story. There are times when it is appropriate to include your "why" in your story and times when it isn't. But identifying and practicing your "why" and connecting it to your end goal will ensure you are ready wherever and whenever the opportunity arises. Later in the book you will read my elevator pitch, which includes my "why." See if you can identify it.

MARKETING YOUR PERSONAL BRAND

Marketing your brand consists of deliberate and strategic actions that help you stand out and showcase your unique strengths, qualities, and experiences. And it doesn't have to cost you an arm and a leg. Thanks to social networking and media platforms, you may not have to retain a high-priced New York or LA marketing firm. With some targeted actions, you can take control of marketing your brand to the people who can help you reach your personal goals or achieve your professional objectives. In the next section, I explain more about some of those actions, beginning with marketing your brand to key stakeholders, or those who can help you achieve your personal or professional goals.

✓ Market your brand to key stakeholders:

- **Boss:** Create opportunities to showcase your strengths, including leading well-structured meetings, managing projects, and organizing networking events.

Example: Leading the marketing communications for Reebok's Rbk signature collection and the global rebranding of Boston Scientific are two examples of how I showcased my organizational and project management strengths. Both opportunities broadened the visibility of my personal brand.

- **Employees:** Demonstrate your self-confidence and commitment to the development of team members by creating opportunities to increase their visibility and promoting their hard work and winning results.

  Example: My team members often presented to and worked directly with senior executives, including the CEO. My project reports and summary e-mails often highlighted the contributions of my staff.

- **Colleagues:** Showcase your organizational skills by being on time for meetings, delivering solid results, and creating a team-focused and collaborative atmosphere.

  Example: Although I led it, the global rebranding of Boston Scientific was supported by a cross-functional team of employees from around the world, leading to the solid execution and well-organized global roll-out of the new brand.

- **Elected officials:** Attend fundraising events, volunteer for political campaigns, and connect with their social media platforms.

  Example: Serving as the campaign chair for Suffolk County (Massachusetts) Sheriff Steve Tompkins during his first-ever run for office, I was able to expose my brand to a new and influential audience.

- **Industry associates:** Join industry-specific groups, be an active participant in social opportunities, and network with key leadership.

Example: Maintaining longtime industry relationships led to my being invited to sit on panels and lead conference sessions, which strengthened my brand and resulted in new business for my company, MDK Brand Management, LLC.

- **Professional organizations:** Sign up with professional organizations, subscribe to newsletters, join their social media sites, and serve on volunteer boards.

    Example: Organizations such as the National Association of Professional Women (NAPW), of which I am a member, help professional women network *with* each other and promote their personal brands *among* each other. I am also on the board of the Greater Boston Chamber of Commerce and served as chair of its Women's Network Advisory Board for two years. Including your affiliation with associations and boards on your biography, résumé, and website (if applicable) could open doors and further establish your brand.

- **Nonprofit/community leaders:** Volunteer for and attend community events, join community boards, donate funds, and explore speaking opportunities.

    Example: Serving on community boards, including Sportsmen's Tennis Club, attending countless events, and networking with community leaders helped develop my leadership skills, increase my visibility, and strengthen my personal brand. This exposure and experience influenced my decision to take the leap of faith and found MDK Brand Management, LLC in 2015.

✓ Leverage opportunities for visibility:

- **Online posts:** Twitter and Instagram are solid platforms to launch and build a strong and visible personal brand. The more active you are, the more visible your brand becomes. It sounds simple, but the 24/7 virtual world can be a challenge.

I have a personal and an MDK account with Twitter (@ dkaigler and @mdkbrandmanage), Facebook, LinkedIn, and Instagram (mdk_brand_management and micheladenise) as well as an MDK website (www.mdkbrandmanagement.com). For this book, I have a Twitter account (@fortydollarsDK), Instagram (fortydollarsmdk), and a website (www. fortydollarsandabrand.com). I also have a YouTube channel. That's numerous platforms that yearn for content.

- **Published articles:** In this day and age, all you need is a social media account to publish articles you author. LinkedIn makes it relatively easy to turn a hobby into a social following. Just make sure to very carefully review or have someone else read your content before sharing it with the world. You'll want to make sure there are no grammatical errors or language that could be perceived as offensive. You might also want to investigate publishing your articles on independent and influential media sites. Although that isn't as easy as pushing them on your own platform, it may be worth the effort.

- **Social media blogs:** Blogging is a great way to network as you develop your brand. Gaining visibility outside of your network could position you and your brand as an expert or thought leader. To accomplish that goal, choose timely, compelling, or relevant topics to write about. Again, be sure to have someone review your content before sharing. Instead of helping your brand, a poorly written blog can easily damage it.

- **Volunteer activities:** Donating your time to a nonprofit organization adds an invaluable layer to your personal brand. It can also form a protective shield around your brand should an inadvertent and unintentional action or behavior threaten to damage it. Volunteer opportunities are never in short supply. Check with nonprofit organizations in your area and ask about events or programs that could use your expertise. I've spent much of my career donating my time and, in many cases, my financial resources to nonprofit organizations. When I launched MDK Brand Management, the nonprofit community supported my brand and my company by giving back to me in the form of new business.

- **Company e-mail updates:** The use of your company's e-mail system should certainly be carefully managed and never exploited for personal gain. However, when you or your team reach a milestone or exceed results, it is acceptable and expected that you share that news with a specific internal group or the entire organization. This is an often overlooked platform when establishing your professional reputation and, by association, your personal brand. Updating the relevant teams or the broad employee base on the projects spearheaded by my team was a staple throughout my corporate career. Such actions engage employees, energize team members, and strengthen personal brands. It's a win-win-win.

- **Work meeting summaries:** We've all been there—sitting through seemingly endless meetings and then unsure of the outcome or never hearing about any follow-up. Your personal brand will benefit greatly by simply distributing a brief note summarizing the meeting, outlining action items, and identifying the owners and due dates. You will be viewed as professional and organized and your team and company will be the ultimate beneficiaries.

- **Networking conversations:** The golf course gets most of the credit but scores of opportunities are also identified during formal and informal, planned and unplanned conversations at networking events or meetings within and outside of your network. Make sure you are ready to convert these conversations into personal brand builders and career makers. In 1990, I was the director of communications for Boys & Girls Clubs of Boston. I was at an event one evening when I met and had an informal conversation with the director of human resources for Reebok. That brief and unexpected moment led to a fantastic seventeen-year Reebok career. As I was setting up MDK Brand Management, I pounded the pavement—pitching to those within my network and

17

FORTY DOLLARS AND A BRAND

meeting those outside of it. In each case, I had to introduce my transition from a corporate leader to an entrepreneur. As a result of this networking investment, I closed out my first full year as a business owner with numerous clients. Never underestimate the power and value of networking.

✓ Create and selectively distribute personal business cards which should include the following:

- Name

- Personal e-mail address

- Personal cell number

- Personal brand buzz words or an inspirational quote

- Your social media sites (e.g. Twitter, Instagram, Facebook, LinkedIn)

When I ask my clients if they have a personal business card, most not only say they don't, but they've never even thought about it. When you're at a networking event and you meet someone with whom you'd like to have a long-term association, you most likely offer your one and only card, the one that includes the name of the company you work for. But what happens if you leave that company and your contact e-mails you? Correct. It bounces back and that connection might be lost forever. I advise my clients to create and carry personal business cards alongside their current employment business cards. Depending on the situation, you can decide which card you want to give up. At least you'll have the choice.

Marketing your personal brand to key stakeholders through your activities and visibility is critical. Ultimately, it is up to you to take control and define how you want to be viewed by others. Don't underestimate the value of getting out, networking, and using those opportunities to help you build your brand and achieve your goals. There are times when the least expected and most amazing opportunities appear as a result of your visibility (e.g., Reebok). And then there are times when you have to create those opportunities through your visibility (e.g., MDK Brand Management). In both cases, you must be prepared to grab those opportunities (along with your personal business card) and maximize them to the fullest.

As you are leveraging your brand to grab and maximize opportunities, watch out for the many roadblocks and potholes that may line your path to awesomeness. Many people encounter challenges or even perhaps a crisis or two while building their brand. I certainly have. Later in the book, I outline some of those challenges and crises my brand faced and the lessons I learned while minimizing or repairing the damage.

There were at least two times in my career when I failed to keep it real, and each nearly cost me dearly. The first time was in the mid-1990s. I was a public relations manager at Reebok and was on my first business trip outside the US. And what a trip it was. I was in charge of managing Reebok's co-sponsorship of The American Ocean's Campaign fundraiser in Los Cabos, Mexico. The organization was founded by actor and environmentalist Ted Danson, who was the event's hospitable host.

I arrived in Los Cabos energized and excited, ready and eager to wax poetic about Reebok's commitment to human rights, while paving the way for the arrival of Reebok executive, Angel Martinez. Shortly after Angel arrived, I introduced him and his wife to the celebrities I'd already met, including Danson and astronaut icon Buzz Aldrin. Pinch me.

The fundraising gala was the stuff dreams are made of. I was seated at one of the main tables and enjoyed the warm temperatures, amazing atmosphere and enthusiastic conversation. At one point, the enthusiasm took over my body like an alien invasion. It all happened so quickly. During the live auction, I seemed to have an out-of-body experience. One of the auction items was a glorious trip with an opening bid of $5,000. Keep in mind that at this point in my career, I was at the manager level, earning a low five-figure salary. I was a wife and mother, with a mortgage and other unavoidable bills. But the alien-probe temporarily erased my memory – my brand - of that reality. I was in an exotic environment, dining amongst diamonds and pearls, Dolce & Gabbana.

I couldn't have been farther away from my world as I sipped champagne and imagined being part of this one. And, then, before I knew it, I flipped up my hand high in the air while holding my large bidding number. In an instant, the auctioneer's confirmation finger pointed in my direction. "Five-thousand dollars!" *Wait, what? Did I just offer to spend thousands of dollars I do not have? On a trip I do not need?* "Five-thousand-dollars going once," said the auctioneer as the gala's minions began surrounding me with their clipboards and payment processing machines. "Five-thousand dollars going twice," said the increasingly confident auctioneer. With my heart wildly pounding inside my chest and my mouth as dry as the Sahara Desert, I was seconds away from disaster. *What was I thinking? This is not my world. I can't afford it!* And it was as if some divine-being decided to save me from myself, a bidding number from across the large outdoor venue flung up the air. "Fifty-five hundred!"

Thank. The. Lord!

The minions and their payment machines disappeared in a flash, as I feigned disappointment and accepted the "oh, Denise, that's too bad" sentiments expressed by my tablemates. I calmly reached for the bottle of wine on the table, filled up my glass and chugged, while silently toasting myself for escaping what would have been the stupidest self-inflicted wound of my career.

A few years later and thousands of miles away, keeping up instead of keeping it real nearly cost me my life. I was on a business trip in Munich, Germany with several Reebok colleagues. One night, we headed to a local pub where we relaxed and enjoyed the local flavor of Munich. After dinner, I was invited to sit at the bar and join the guys in a tequila face-off. Without thinking it through, I accepted the challenge and took my place at the bar. It was stupid, I know. But I was one of the few African American female leaders at Reebok and felt the irrational need to prove myself as "one of the guys."

Less than thirty minutes later, I had kept up with the guys and thrown back 10 (that's ten) straight shots of tequila! I had never done anything like that before and didn't even really enjoy the taste of straight tequila. It wasn't who I was. But my own identity was less important than being accepted by my co-workers.

I was starting to feel sick and didn't want the guys to see that side of me. So, with my head spinning, I clumsily stepped down from the bar stool and stumbled my way to the pool room in the back of the bar. Before I knew it, more than an hour had passed. I was still tipsy and very tired. I just wanted to get to the hotel and fall into my bed. I walked back to the main pub area and looked around for my Reebok colleagues. They weren't there! The bartender told me that the guys thought I'd left already and they headed back to the hotel. *What!* I was all alone in a bar in Munich, Germany. And I don't speak German. It was about 2am. I figured I would walk outside and take a cab back to the hotel. But there were no cabs in sight! I walked around for what felt like an eternity. Nothing. *Now, I'm getting scared.* Everyone I saw on the street only spoke German. It didn't help that I was probably slurring my words as I tried to explain my predicament. I didn't know what to do. And I didn't remember the name or the address of the hotel. I was completely lost. I was exposed and worried about my safety. I had no weapon, nothing to protect me from a random act of violence. *Wow, this is not happening.*

23

Once again, my guardian angel stepped in and a cab suddenly appeared. I hailed it and jumped in without hesitation. And, thankfully, the driver spoke English! But he wasn't a mind reader. As I fumbled to recall the name and description of the hotel, the driver asked if I had the envelop with the room key. Ah, yes! And as expected, the hotel's name and address were printed on the front. Within 15 minutes, I was grateful to be safe and sound inside my room. But I wasn't grateful for the tequila still ripping apart my stomach and swirling inside my head. I spent the next few hours slumped over my toilet seat and cursing my need to keep up with the boys.

Although these two experiences occurred decades ago, the lesson I learned remains astonishingly clear. Never, ever pretend to be someone you're not. Always be yourself. The exhilaration associated with "keeping up" is fleeting. The benefit of "keeping it real" lasts a lifetime and ensures the authenticity of your personal brand.

CHAPTER 4

REBOOTING AFTER CAREER DETOUR

One day, you're sailing along, enjoying calm seas and seemingly endless sunshine. Cloud Nine is under your feet and a lucrative wind is beneath your wings. Then suddenly, life happens.

Most of us have been through some sort of career detour: a job elimination, layoff or termination or a planned or forced retirement. Perhaps your company has relocated you to an unfamiliar city or you're transitioning to an entirely new industry. Or maybe you are simply in need of a change. There are countless examples of professional shifts that warrant a personal brand reboot: A former athlete who wants to become a wealth and investment manager, a former police officer who wants to become a social worker, a former television reporter who wants to become a corporate leader or a former corporate executive who wants to become a business owner.

In May of 2011, I was hired by Boston Scientific Corporation as its senior vice president of corporate communications. In June of 2015, my role was eliminated as part of a corporate reorganization. The internal email from my boss was very complimentary. The following is an excerpt: "Since joining Boston Scientific 4 years ago, Denise has led the enhancement of our Corporate Intranet site, strengthened our media relationships, launched our new Boston Scientific brand, led the creation of our corporate brand declaration 'Advancing science for life,' established new video production capabilities, revitalized the Corporate Citizenship group, spearheaded the Corporate Crisis Protocol, and recently launched the Lives Transformed program. Denise has also been an unwavering supporter of our Bridge Employee Resource Group, serving as a mentor to several Bridge members."

Nice way to go out, right? Absolutely! So, now what? After more than 20 years in corporate, was my destiny determined? How much would this professional change impact my personal brand?

For many of us, losing a job is part of the employment experience. Chances are that at one point in your career, you have been - or will be - laid off. According to the LA Times, between 2009 and 2014, one-fifth of the US labor force was laid off. Company restructuring happens, positions are eliminated. It seems few are immune.

Whether your life's change is due to a layoff, retirement, relocation, graduation or career transition, the key is to view it as an opportunity to reset your course and reboot your brand. But before you can reset your course, you must first identify the course you want to navigate and then outline any obstacles standing in your way. What do you want to do? Are there any obstacles blocking that path? Do you need to go back to school? Do you need a license or a certificate? If you were a corporate executive before being let go, will you be able to re-enter the corporate world at a managerial level or will you need to climb your way back up? If your goal is to enter an entirely new industry, how will you get your foot in the door? These are among the critical questions to answer. But the most critical question is how do you now want to define your new brand?

After my job elimination, I found my face pressed firmly against the challenge of rebooting my brand. I set my eyes on realizing my long-held and boxed-up dream of entrepreneurship. And for that, I needed my network to look beyond the corporate executive -- to see past the glitz and glam of working with athletes and celebrities, and flying on corporate jets. It may sound easy, but rebooting a brand is hard work that requires determination and a thick skin. Although it may have taken you decades to establish your professional reputation and build your personal brand, you most likely have only a few months to define and recreate your brand so you can effectively and quickly begin tapping into your broad network. And there is no guarantee that will happen. The occasional kick in the stomach during your reboot may slow you down, but don't let it knock you out.

Below are the recommended steps to take to reboot your brand, and what I did to reboot mine:

1. Make a decision: Decide what you want, not what others expect. I was emphatic about and comfortable with my decision to leave corporate and start MDK Brand Management, LLC. I understood the difficult task ahead. Still, I did not waver.

2. Define your new look: Once you've made the decision about how you want to move forward after experiencing a life or career detour, take a fresh look at your 'look.' This includes reevaluating your wardrobe (do you need to start or stop wearing business suits?), testing a new hairstyle, or even wearing different jewelry. Consider any change that helps you feel more excited about your brand reboot. As for me, I changed my hairstyle (went natural) and stored most of my business suits.

3. Control the message: I never minced words or let others tell my story. I was direct and honest about losing my corporate job and going out on my own. In addition to building credibility, being candid puts you in control of your message.

4. Activate your network: Being out and about is less about fun and more about business. Introducing my new brand at social and professional events, increasing my engagement on existing boards and joining new boards, sitting on panels and speaking at conferences proved effective. Whether or not you enjoy it, networking is absolutely necessary.

5. Distribute branded collateral: Gone were the days of my name followed by an impressive title and the logo of a multi-billion-dollar global entity on my business card. The MDK branded materials I distributed at every opportunity included my photo and description and the name of my new company. It was a worthwhile investment. The investment you make in your future may also prove worthwhile.

6. Develop marketing platforms: It took time and focus but my business websites, mdkbrandmanagement.com and fortydollarsandabrand.com, along with my Twitter, Instagram, LinkedIn, Facebook and YouTube platforms, solidified my new brand and communicated my shift from corporate executive to brand strategist and business owner.

7. Project new personal brand: I defined my inspirational "why" and wrote my entrepreneur-focused elevator pitch. Although many still recall my Reebok days (I left the company in 2008), founding MDK Brand Management and rebooting my brand was one of the best business decisions I have ever made. Don't hesitate. Go for it!

The overall key to a seamless transition and brand reboot is making a firm decision to embrace the opportunities that await. Hold your head high and move forward with enthusiasm and resolve. And if you see an unsettling blow heading in your direction, stiffen your chin, look the challenge in the eye and absorb the hit. Not only will your reaction not deliver the desired satisfaction, it will embolden you and energize your next move.

Whatever the change that has suddenly thrusted you into the camp of Brand Reboot, it will benefit you to first explore the landscape that awaits. For instance, if you've been laid off from a retail sales job and want to switch it up and transition to a human resources role, do your research. What are the personal attributes that can help someone thrive in the HR field? What are the educational requirements? What type of personal brand does it take to grow in that field? Look through online resources such as Glassdoor, LinkedIn, Indeed and others for helpful tips and advice. Once you understand the requirements, consider the following:

- Rework resume, include summary or profile
- Include relevant buzz words in resume and cover letter
- Write/update your elevator pitch
- Join relevant LinkedIn groups
- Activate professional memberships

- Attend networking events
- Update social media profiles
- Create personal business cards/other collateral

Before you head out to introduce your rebooted brand, strengthen your network by joining a board, increasing memberships, or taking on volunteer assignments. Make sure you understand and are speaking the relevant jargon or lingo, and are familiar with the news and other details impacting or influencing the new industry you want to pursue. And as you're updating your resume and writing your rebooted elevator pitch, ask yourself the following questions:

> - What do I want to accomplish during the next 5, 10 or 20 years?
> - What kind of impact do I want to have on the current or next generation?
> - Do I want to work full-time, part-time or not at all?
> - Do I want to focus on the nonprofit or for-profit space?
> - What makes me happy?
> - What makes me unhappy?
> - Have I ever wanted to start a business?
> - How much longer do I need to work?
> - Do I want to stay in my current industry? Or transition to another one?
> - What three words best describe me?
> - How do people define me today?
> - How do I want to be defined after my brand reboot?

If you choose to reboot your brand following a planned or unplanned change in your life or career, consider conducting a personal analysis of your SWOT (Strengths, Weaknesses, Opportunities and Threats). See the SWOT Analysis Worksheet, courtesy of mindtools.com. Take a few moments to complete the worksheet as the first step to rebooting your personal brand.

SWOT ANALYSIS WORKSHEET

STRENGTHS
List what you do well

1.

2.

3.

4.

WEAKNESSES
List what you need to improve

1.

2.

3.

4.

OPPORTUNITIES
List external factors
positively impacting your career

1.

2.

3.

4.

THREATS
List of external factors
negatively impacting your career

1.

2.

3.

4.

If you need more space, use the full-page forms on the following pages.

STRENGTHS
List what you do well

WEAKNESSES
List what you need to improve

OPPORTUNITIES
List external factors positively impacting your career

THREATS
List of external factors negatively impacting your career

Okay. So, you've done some self-reflecting. Now what? Turn your self-reflection into actionable strategies. What will you do to leverage your strengths, address your weaknesses, and use the opportunities to counter the threats? And how will all of this work to your advantage when rebooting your brand? The key is to make sure that you're not just making a list that will sit inside this book, never to be seen again. Make it work for you.

ACTIONABLE STRATEGIES
Turn your SWOT into action. What will you do? Make a list.

Self-awareness - being aware of your strengths, weaknesses, opportunities and threats - will help you not only effectively reboot your brand, but ensure that your rebooted brand is authentic. The key to conducting an analysis of your SWOT is to be honest with yourself so others believe in you and your new brand.

Launching a new career after years in another one is more common than you may think. And starting a company is also fairly popular, especially among baby-boomers. Entrepreneurship is statistically more common among older men and women. According to the Harvard Business School, "the highest rate of entrepreneurship in the US has been among 55 to 64 year olds, and people over 55 are twice as likely to launch successful new companies than those in the 20 to 34 age group." This, of course, is due to the experience that people collect over their careers, and the expertise with which they can speak on a subject. The founders of McDonald's, Coca Cola, and KFC were all over the age of 50 when they established their businesses.

It's not the age, it's the vision. As long as you have a clear vision of what you want your rebooted brand to represent, you're on your way.

Networking is also a necessity. One of the most helpful components of my brand reboot was serving on boards. I serve on the Greater Boston Chamber of Commerce board and the University of Massachusetts Boston advisory board. I sourced those critical networks to fuel my transition from a corporate executive to a small business entrepreneur. It was a new and exhilarating experience to introduce myself as the head of my own company. Through my board exposure, I met fellow corporate leaders and entrepreneurs, and began establishing relationships that were based on my expertise, not on a corporate employer's brand recognition.

Continually marketing my rebooted brand helped relegate the role of my prior global employers to background information which strengthened my credibility. People began to see the value in what I was saying and the expertise I was sharing to help strengthen and enhance others. I was not defined by a large global company but, rather, by my own strengths and contributions.

While networking and marketing are critical when rebooting your brand, much of your reboot triumph is contingent upon your mindset. Confidence, follow-through and diligence will help your rebooted brand take hold and flourish. In addition, finding motivation through an inspirational word or phrase can also help energize your rebooted brand. The tagline for my company, MDK Brand Management, is "Enhancing Brands. Creating Opportunities." I love this tagline for my company. However, I am still motivated by the personal brand sound-bite I've embraced for more than two decades: "Denise gets sh*t done." Without a doubt, this phrase expresses the goal and mission of my rebooted brand following the detour of my career.

What words express the goal of your rebooted brand?

CHAPTER 5

CREATING AN ENTREPRENEUR-BRAND

Whether you're a future, recent or seasoned entrepreneur, your personal brand is critical to your company's image. According to entrepreneur.com, *"Your personal brand is your calling card for attracting like-minded people who will believe in your message. Whether you are a freelancer, startup or you just received your first round of financing, the effort you put into your personal brand directly affects how others perceive the value of your business."*

You absolutely must build and maintain a visible entrepreneur-brand if you're going to build and maintain your business. And make no mistake, that will take time and a lot of work. For those who dislike being out and about, shaking hands and smiling until your face freezes, get over it! That's exactly what you'll be doing. That is, if you want your business to make money.

As I tell my MDK Brand Management clients, branding is a business. And like a business, some thrive, some do not. When building your entrepreneur-brand, find a strategy that works for you. Perhaps operating on a set schedule is your chosen strategy. For example, on Monday, update your social media sites; Tuesday, connect with business contacts; Wednesday, send out 'thank you' notes; Thursday, practice your elevator pitch, and on Friday, attend a networking event. And don't forget to take care of yourself. Appearance matters. Remember to exercise, keep your nails clean and keep your hair kept and neat. This strategy will help establish your brand as a diligent, thoughtful and hardworking entrepreneur.

As you're transitioning to your entrepreneur-brand, think about the values that are important to you and how you will infuse those values into your company. Also, remember why you founded your company. Write down the story that led to its creation. Finally, people are attracted to those with whom they can relate. What's relatable about your personal brand that can be reflected throughout your new business? Your personal brand should align with the brand of your new business. There should be alignment between the goals and values of your company and you. Your company's tagline should also be a statement in which you personally believe. As its leader, you are your company.

Right after I made the decision to transition from corporate leader to small business owner, one actionable piece of advice I received was to journal, to keep a living record of the entire process of my career transition and personal brand reboot. I heeded the advice. May 27, 2015 was the day before my last physical day at Boston Scientific. Since that day, I've been documenting the highs - and lows - of becoming and being an entrepreneur.

Less than four weeks after leaving Boston Scientific, I founded my limited liability company, MDK Brand Management. Even though my business was named, the logo was created and the entity was filed and trademarked, I still had my share of doubters. Some thought I wasn't serious about transitioning my brand and managing a business. In a sense, I understood the doubt. I'd been working at large companies for most of my career. With paychecks arriving on a regular basis, I didn't have to worry about how the bills would be paid. And if you know about starting a business, there are few days, if any, when 'worry' doesn't rear its ugly head.

Although I was nervous about giving up the pay-day security, in my gut, I knew I was on the right path. Too many stars were aligned for it not to work. Doubt if you must, but I firmly believe that when making a major life change, one's gut is often a reliable barometer. And my gut has never let me down.

CHAPTER 6

REBUILDING A DAMAGED BRAND

Lately, there appears to be no shortage of self-inflicted wounds to personal brands and, as a result, damaged careers and ruined livelihoods. The #MeToo, #TimesUp and other galvanizing movements have unearthed damaging behaviors and actions by celebrities, politicians and other influencers, that were, to most of the clueless public, shocking and jaw-dropping.

I often tell my MDK Brand Management clients that unless you're dead, damaged brands can be repaired. However, I do believe there are rare exceptions to this belief. For instance, I do not believe the world will ever embrace the man whose simulated Brooklyn, New York brownstone became the Thursday night home for many of us. My goodness, what happened, Dr. Huxtable? Where did things go so terribly wrong? I have serious doubts that there is a path forward for Bill Cosby to regain the beloved brand that, for eight years, practically defined family values.

There are countless men and women who dealt with or are dealing with a personal or a professional crisis, perhaps of their own making. Although there are many more and worse repercussions than an irreparable or severely damaged brand, that is the focus of this chapter. It would be normal for someone caught up in a crisis, especially a public-facing one, to retain the services of legal counsel. But there is another critical element that should be part of that protective, supportive shield. If you find yourself embroiled in a personal or professional crisis, it is certainly wise to keep an eye on the possible legal impact. The other eye should be focused on maintaining or rebuilding your career. And the first step is to rebuild your personal brand.

In my company's MDK Brand Management workshops, I sometimes ask participants to Google a celebrity and present a summary of their findings. During a brand management session with employees from a corporate client, the Google exercise focused on several individuals whose brands were under assault, including political staffer Huma Abedin, former wife of Anthony Weiner. It seems we've come to know this notable figure more through her marriage to Weiner and employment by Hillary Clinton. Despite her own credentials that include graduating from George Washington University and working her way up from a West Wing intern to trusted advisor to Secretary Clinton, do we really know Abedin's brand? To paraphrase Amazon founder Jeff Bezos, your personal brand is what people say about you when you're not in the room. In Abedin's case, what do people say about her when she's not in the room? Unfortunately, the answer from many of us would probably not be preferred by Abedin. And therein lies the challenge and importance of defining your own personal brand. It is up to you to project and market your brand in ways that ensure it is not tied up or held down by someone else's, whether that brand is positive, negative, or neutral.

Another branding challenge involves going underground following a hurtful, harmful, or painful experience. I understand. Sometimes, we all need a moment; time to reflect, reassess, and rethink life's purpose. If you find yourself in this position and are then ready to reemerge and reconnect with the civilized world, resist the temptation to showcase your pain and broadcast your disappointment. Hold your head high, even if it makes you dizzy. Smile from ear to ear, even if it locks your jaw. Extend your hand and shake others' firmly, even if it kills you. It isn't how hard you fall, it's how confidently you get up and move on. That will define and strengthen your brand more than you can imagine.

While you're defining and strengthening your personal brand, you must also be sure to protect it from those who want to control or damage it. Exposing your brand in ways that allow it to be defined or shaped by uncontrollable factors, especially social media, can have devastating results. A hiring manager may Google your name before extending a job offer. A potential love interest may study your profile on a dating site before sending that 'hang-out' text. Manage your personal brand on all platforms, real and virtual, so no one can rob you of your awesomeness.

There are numerous examples of people who, in a careless moment, have inadvertently found themselves regretting eternal notoriety rather than enjoying short-lived fame. Justine Sacco, the PR executive who tweeted about being protected from AIDS while in South Africa because she was white, was forever memorialized by tons of negative media coverage, including the excruciating February 12, 2015, *New York Times* story, "How One Stupid Tweet Blew Up Justine Sacco's Life." If a PR executive can shoot herself in the foot, it can happen to anyone.

Before you tap that key that will either launch your brand into social media heaven or hell, think through the potential impact of your post, both negative and positive. As importantly and if possible, have someone listen to the idea first. You might also consider writing the post, sleeping on it, then reading it again the next day. Chances are you will rewrite or tweak it, or perhaps delete it entirely.

A social media blunder is just one example of how a personal brand can spiral out of control and into a crisis. You might recall the media storm that engulfed US swimmer and Olympic gold medalist Ryan Lochte. In 2016, Lochte's personal brand sank to the bottom of the pool amid accusations that he lied about being robbed at gunpoint while at the Olympics in Rio de Janeiro, Brazil. And remember Billy Bush, the former entertainment reporter and *TODAY Show* personality who was fired weeks after the release of a controversial 2005 video in which Bush is heard laughing along as Donald Trump makes disparaging comments about women? Bush had created a solid, affable personal brand that seemed to be enjoyed and supported by millions of women. So, when those same women were outraged by the tape and Bush's role on it, the hit to his personal brand was all but assured. The only question was how hard of a hit would his brand take. *Entertainment Tonight* reported that Bush hired a public relations crisis management company to help guide him through the crisis. One factor that undoubtedly helped soothe his pain was a reported $10 million settlement from NBC. It's not clear how, when, where, or even whether Bush will publicly resurface. But if and when he does, I imagine his new brand will reflect the hard and painful lessons he learned.

If your brand has been battered, bruised or completely ripped to shreds, by either your own hand or someone else's, repair and recovery is possible. But you have to remain focused and be committed to the long-term process. If you are responsible for damaging your personal brand, here are several pointers to help rebuild it:

1. Admit (to yourself) the damage to your personal brand

2. Accept your role in creating or exacerbating the damage

3. Apologize to anyone involved, impacted or hurt

4. Avoid being in the spotlight for a brief period

5. Author a book, blogs or articles reclaiming your particular expertise

6. Arm yourself with an impassioned, thoughtful elevator pitch

7. Attend social and professional events, and revive your network

8. Arrange individual meetings to marshal supporters and advocates

9. Believe that you deserve another chance to live your awesomeness

10. Be awesome again

By learning tough lessons after a hard fall and being committed to repairing the damage, your brand can survive and your journey can continue.

The following chapter recounts twenty stories from my brand-building days of overcoming challenges and defying the odds as a television news reporter and then in corporate at Reebok, Rockport, Nintendo, and Boston Scientific. At the beginning of each story, I share a tip I learned while in the trenches. I hope you find these tips helpful to keeping your personal brand on a steady incline and tilted toward your awesomeness.

CHAPTER 7

DEFYING THE ODDS
TWENTY MDK BRANDING TIPS AND STORIES FROM THE TRENCHES

From the time I was a kid, I was constantly hearing that I couldn't and that I wouldn't. I was a poor African American girl with crooked teeth and bad skin, trying to make it out and up. The odds were stacked against me, and I had no evidence to prove otherwise. In fact, I was convinced the predictions would prove to be true. I had no persona and no voice. I was Ralph Ellison's *Invisible Man*—I didn't exist in the real world. Back then, a personal brand was as foreign to me as a trip to the moon. But I soon learned the importance of defining and marketing a strong personal brand to open the doors that were not only closed, but dead-bolted shut.

The following twenty tips and stories reflect and recount some of my amazing, exciting and, at times, sobering experiences during my career. I hope you find the stories engaging and the tips helpful as you develop, manage, and market your personal brand while navigating challenges and opportunities during your career and life journey.

***

MDK BRAND TIP #1: YES YOU CAN!
Life happens. The brand you have today need not be your brand tomorrow. With an open mind and positive attitude, you can leverage inevitable changes in your life to evolve your personal brand in definitive and purposeful ways.

LEANING IN

After graduating from Emerson College in Boston and with my teeth straightened by braces I funded through part-time jobs, I arrived in Columbus, Georgia, for my first on-air news reporting job. "Denise Moore, reporting for Channel 38, WLTZ-TV." Nine months later, on September 6, 1986, I married Joe Kaigler, the man I'd been dating for less than a year. We'd met in Boston and were engaged three months later. Life was a whirlwind. This news reporter/newlywed soon faced a decision many newly married career women face: Do I keep my maiden name or switch to my married name? Or do I keep both— Kaigler for official private business and Moore for my public persona? I decided to go all in. I would begin evolving my brand by becoming Denise Kaigler, both privately and publicly.

Just a few months after Joe "put a ring on it" and returning to my reporter job in Columbus, I decided to lean into married life. I moved back to Boston to make a home with my new husband.

The first several weeks back in Boston were awful. I resented my husband and wasn't happy with my life. Thankfully, a friend helped me land immediately at Boston's Channel 7, where he worked. Although my new gig, a production assistant, wasn't on air, at least it was in the television industry. For that, I was grateful. After all, it was unrealistic of me to expect to be hired as a reporter in a top-ten market after just one year working in a very small market. I also recognized that learning the behind-the-scenes of television news could prove incredibly beneficial to my reporting career. Even with this awareness, I struggled with the sudden halt of my on-air work. Instead of being a reporter, I was a production assistant, then later an ENG coordinator, the person responsible for making sure the reporters' news stories were edited and ready for the newscasts.

As a newly married woman, transitioning from Miss Moore to Mrs. Kaigler, and setting up a one-bedroom apartment in Boston, I should have been walking on clouds. But I couldn't help but feel like I was living in purgatory. Clearly, that wasn't a sustainable mindset. To quote Maya Angelou, "If you don't like something, change it. If you can't change it, change your attitude." And that's exactly what I did. I couldn't change that I was no longer a TV news reporter, but I could change my attitude about the opportunity to carve out a new career path. In 1989, I continued the evolution of my brand by transitioning from television news to the public relations and communications industry. At the time, I didn't realize the significance of that transition. Landing my first post-TV job as the director of communications for Boys & Girls Clubs of Boston changed my entire life. That job led to my 24-year career climbing the corporate ladder.

***

> MDK BRAND TIP #2: REMEMBER WHO YOU ARE
>
> While the story below represents the extreme end of mischaracterization, many of us have experienced some level of profiling. If this happens to you, keep your cool, explain who you are, and try to calmly set the record straight.

YOU THOUGHT I WAS *WHAT?*

Shortly after being promoted to senior manager of corporate communications for Reebok, I was tasked with being the media spokesperson for the company's highly visible Reebok Human Rights Program. After making a few media comments for stories about footwear factories in Asia, I decided to take a chance and suggest to Reebok's head of manufacturing that I visit the footwear factories and see the conditions for myself. Doing so might strengthen my spokesperson credibility and, more importantly, I would feel more confident about my public comments. The executive agreed and sponsored my trip.

My week in Ho Chi Minh City, Vietnam, was both fascinating and frightening. The food, the historic sites, the people, and the culture were all unlike anything I had ever experienced before in my life. But there was one particular experience that left me reeling.

Shawn was an executive for Reebok Vietnam and my hospitable host. Each morning, he picked me up from the hotel and took me to the office and then a Reebok-subcontracted footwear factory. Each element of our daily schedule was carefully planned. One morning, a knock on my hotel room door caught me by surprise. It was the hotel manager. This was definitely not in the plan. I opened the door, something I probably shouldn't have done. The manager pushed inside my room. With a firm voice, he demanded to know the identity of the "white man" who was picking me up in the lobby every day. My head was spinning. The manager went on to tell me that the hotel did not want "that kind of activity" taking place in his hotel. What activity? I told him that I worked for Reebok and was in Vietnam on company business, which included visiting footwear manufacturing facilities. *Was this really happening?* I was in a foreign country, alone in my hotel room, being strong-armed by a hotel official. My best defense at that defenseless moment was to defend myself with details. As tempting as it was, this wasn't the time to stand on my soapbox and angrily affirm my US citizenship and proclaim my right to privacy. When the manager realized how deeply frightened his presence made me, he turned and left.

When Shawn arrived a short time later, I could hardly contain myself. The second after I finished recounting my ordeal, he answered the nagging question still swirling inside my head: What activity was the manager talking about? Once Shawn said the words, it was so obviously clear. The manager assumed I was a prostitute and Shawn was my john. Wow, that was a first. Why, I wondered. It was the mid-1990s. Shawn told me that an African American woman with a white man in Vietnam could only mean one thing since a businesswoman who looked like me was a rare sight there. Despite this unfortunate incident, I still view Vietnam as one of the most amazing places I have ever been fortunate to visit.

***

> ## MDK BRAND TIP #3: MAINTAIN YOUR INTEGRITY
>
> Never let anyone rob you of your integrity. If you work for a company and protecting that company's brand is among your primary responsibilities, take that role seriously. If you find yourself in a situation where that responsibility creates a conflict, you can either make a call to your supervisor (if there's time), or go with your gut and hope the brass has your back. If you go with your gut, make sure you're able to clearly justify your decision based on your primary role and responsibilities. Your commitment to protecting your company's brand may not only protect your personal brand, it could save your job!

MY DAMAGED BRAND

My unwavering protection of Reebok's brand was, at times, harmful to my own personal brand. And make no mistake, your company's brand and your personal brand are sometimes intertwined. I will always remember a phone call that I wish I could take back. I had spearheaded several parties to market Reebok's Rbk signature collection and was tasked with planning another bash with a well-known celebrity in a major market. During the planning call, the celebrity's team began to frame the focus of the party around that celebrity. I made a statement that resulted in total silence on the phone. It was something along the lines that the party was about the Reebok brand, not about that celebrity. There was definitely a subtler way to make the point.

I could only imagine what happened after that call ended. Because the next call to my office was to inform me that I was being removed from the Rbk party team. It didn't matter that this was a marketing platform I helped conceptualize in partnership with an executive from Interscope Records who was retained as a marketing consultant for Reebok.

I stood by my statement, although I could have used more tact. The Reebok brand was the main focus of these events. While the celebrities were critical to drawing strong attendance, generating media coverage, and creating massive buzz throughout the urban and investment communities, we could not lose sight of our primary objective. I took that responsibility very seriously.

A male marketing vice president at Reebok was put in charge of the Rbk parties. A simultaneous kick in the teeth and punch in the stomach would have hurt less. Reebok had begun to build its cool factor among the coveted urban male and young female demographic. So, my prompt removal from the Rbk team hurt. But the pain didn't last. Toward the end of the Rbk party I wasn't allowed to manage but invited to attend, the marketing VP now in charge approached me as I stood outside for some fresh air. To my surprise, he handed the Rbk party reins back over to me. I gladly accepted, relieved that my celebrity faux pas had not eclipsed my defined brand of getting the job done.

That wasn't my first controversial encounter with a celebrity that damaged by personal brand while I was protecting the Reebok brand. That distinction goes to the conflict I had with an entertainment mogul I will refer to as Mr. X. Thanks to the Interscope Records executive paving the way, I went to New York for an introductory meeting with Mr. X in his office. During the meeting, we discussed the possibility of Reebok signing him as a celebrity endorser. My first near-fatal move was my pompous, self-congratulatory e-mail summarizing that meeting. It was an e-mail I should have never written and certainly should have never sent. My brand definitely took a hit as a result of that message.

In the midst of collaboration discussions between Reebok and Mr. X, I needed to go to Paris, France, for the Track & Field World Championships. As I boarded the flight, my cell rang. It was Mr. X. We spoke for a few moments. I committed to him that I would connect with Reebok CEO Paul Fireman when I came back to the States. A few days after I returned to my Reebok office, the unthinkable happened. Just before Reebok was to pull the trigger with Mr. X, he signed a short-term agreement with Nike. I couldn't believe it. I went to Paul and strongly recommended we not go through with the deal. I expressed my concern that we would be signing a celebrity who just inked a deal with our archrival. We would be viewed as just a check, not a brand that was truly valued and respected by the celebrity. Paul agreed. My role in killing the deal between Reebok and Mr. X nearly killed my personal brand and my Reebok career. Mr. X was outraged. But Paul understood that I was simply doing everything I could to protect the Reebok brand. And for that, he protected mine.

I needed Paul's protection one more time following a near-fatal encounter with another celebrity. This time, it was at an Rbk party with a music producer I'll refer to as Mr. O. Reebok had partnered with Mr. O to host the Rbk party in his hometown. I was backstage with other members of the planning team getting ready to kick off the event. Mr. O entered the area, nicely dressed in a very cool outfit. Checking him out, I worked my way down to his feet, and nearly fell to mine. Mr. O was wearing Nikes! Once again, in hindsight, I could have and should have handled the situation differently. But my frustration got the better of me. I asked Mr. O what he was thinking when he got dressed to host a Reebok event and decided to put on a pair of Nike kicks. He said they matched his outfit. *Wait. What? Seriously?* I firmly asked Mr. O to go back to his room, remove his Nikes, and put on the Reebok shoes he was given. Unless he did that, he was not going to host the Reebok party.

Mr. O complied. He came back a few minutes later wearing his fresh new Reebok sneakers. The party went on as planned.

A couple of days later, something happened that I hadn't planned or expected. I was reprimanded for apparently embarrassing the producer and another music executive who was backstage. I felt sick to my stomach. *What did I just do to my reputation, to my personal brand?* I was a hard worker and worried that somehow that would be lost in this kafuffle. I wanted desperately to turn back the clock, to rewind the moment. I mentally begged for a redo. Imagine how many personal brands would benefit from such a matrix. Although I was worried about my own personal brand, I did not feel badly about giving Mr. O the ultimatum in my quest to protect Reebok's Rbk brand. However, I did not intend to anger, upset, or embarrass anyone else and, for that, I felt badly. I called the embarrassed executive and apologized, not knowing whether such a move would restore my brand to health. I just could not let Mr. O walk out on that Reebok stage wearing Nike shoes. I would not be doing my job if I allowed that to happen. The executive understood, although I think he was still a little salty about the entire episode.

I never saw or spoke with Mr. O again.

***

> ## MDK BRAND TIP #4: SURROUND YOURSELF WITH BELIEVERS
> Make sure you are around people who believe in you, who support you, and who nudge you outside of your comfort zone and toward your awesomeness.

BEYONCÉ, HALLE, NATALIE, OPRAH, AND ME—OH MY!

The Carousel of Hope Ball is a celebrity-rich gala that raises funds to fight childhood diabetes. The event was created by billionaires Marvin and Barbara Davis, whose young daughter was diagnosed with diabetes. Back then, childhood diabetes was a relatively unknown disease, which meant little to no public funds were being raised.

In the summer of 2004, Reebok's LA-based celebrity PR agency and two of its executives arranged for me to have lunch with Barbara Davis in Beverly Hills to learn more about the event. After being inspired by the organization's mission and in complete and thorough awe of Mrs. Davis, I agreed to recommend to my boss that Reebok join the gala as a major sponsor. We did.

The sixteenth annual star-studded extravaganza was held at the Beverly Hilton a few months later, on October 23. Although I had been to LA numerous times and attended several black-tie events, this particular evening had me feeling like Cinderella going to her first ball.

While working the main room alongside my dear friend and Reebok's LA entertainment consultant Carl Bendix, we were reminded of the VIP reception taking place in the next room. When Carl and I entered the room, we immediately noticed the bevy of beauties behind a red rope and surrounded by a throng of paparazzi flashing their cameras. Carl grabbed my hand and ushered me closer to the group.

"You should be in that photo," Carl whispered to me.

"What are you talking about? I can't do that. Look who's *in* that photo!" Halle Berry, Beyoncé, Natalie Cole, Oprah, and Mrs. Davis were on full display.

After Carl and I went back and forth a couple of rounds, I began to believe that it was possible for me to be in that shot. Reebok was a main sponsor, our logo was on the backdrop behind that group of beautiful people, and I was the only Reebok representative in attendance.

With Carl's encouragement, I took a deep breath and approached the tuxedo-attired defense guarding the roped-off entrance. I soon saw that it was Reebok's LA PR agency rep.

Perfect.

After the rep and I greeted each other, I went for it. "That's a great photo opp. I'd like to get in it. Can you please let me through?"

When I saw his momentary hesitation, it was time for a frank reminder.

"You know that Reebok is a sponsor of this gala. Our logo is on the backdrop. And since I'm the Reebok representative here, I'd appreciate being allowed to be in that amazing shot. Please."

After checking with Mrs. Davis and getting the okay, the rep allowed me to join the celebrity circle. As if that wasn't enough of a mind-blow, the ultimate out-of-this-world unthinkable happened. Somehow, I ended up in the center of the photo, in the middle of Beyoncé, Halle, Natalie, Oprah, and Barbara. Oh. My. Goodness!

That evening in LA was one of the most exciting and unforgettable experiences of my career and my entire life. That one moment injected in my veins a level of poise I had never before felt or projected. I would never have had the courage to step inside that circle and on top of that mountain had it not been for Carl, someone who had more confidence in me than I had in myself. It was the tipping point of my personal brand. Here I come, awesomeness!

Believing is seeing: Beyoncé, Halle Berry, Denise, Natalie Cole, Oprah, and Barbara Davis at the Carousel of Hope Ball, Los Angeles, CA

> ## MDK BRAND TIP #5: BELIEVE YOU BELONG
>
> Resist the urge to doubt that you belong in an upscale situation or swanky environment. It is easy to let your mind wander to a place of doubt about your place in the universe. It may be scary, but you belong anywhere your path in life leads you. Project your confidence, demonstrate your command, and keep repeating in your mind: I got this!

MR. KATZENBERG WILL SEE YOU NOW

I couldn't believe that I was being escorted to the office of Jeffrey Katzenberg, president of DreamWorks Studios. Wow, me! This shy, former buck-toothed, skinny, pimple-prone girl from S.E., DC was about to sit in the office of one of the most powerful men in Hollywood, if not the entertainment world. My Reebok bosses were considering my recommendation to sign up as a corporate sponsor of the "Night Before the Oscars" gala. But before making a decision, they wanted me to request and be granted a private meeting with Mr. Katzenberg.

When I checked in at my LA hotel, I was greeted with details of my meeting. Even the details were exciting. I was to go to DreamWorks Studios, where I would be picked up in a golf cart and whisked off to the executive offices on the studio lot. I'd seen movies where people whirl about in those carts but never, ever had I imagined I would be one of those people.

After a surprisingly short wait, I was taken to Mr. Katzenberg's office. He stood and politely greeted me. To this day, I wonder if he wondered what the heck I was doing in his office. He wanted Reebok to come in as a major sponsor of the pre-Oscars bash. I had my marching orders in my head and knew what I could say yes to and when I had to reply, "Let us think about it and I'll get back to you."

The good news was that I was able to leave thirty minutes later with a deal that made both parties happy. Several weeks later, I was one of ten Reebok leaders attending the "Night Before the Oscars" bash. It was one of the most magical experiences of my career. I met and chatted with numerous celebrities, including Martin Lawrence, Jennifer Aniston, Richard Gere, Harrison Ford, Calista Flockhart, and Courteney Cox. In addition to attending the "Night Before the Oscars," I have twice attended the Oscars' Academy Awards ceremony. Twenty years ago, I could never have imagined that the invisible Denise Moore would find her voice, strengthen her confidence, and become the brand of Denise Kaigler who was now in the midst of Hollywood A-listers. I not only believed I belonged, here I was.

***

MDK BRAND TIP #6: STAY STRONG WHEN THE GOING GETS TOUGH

How we manage the ups and downs of life has a direct impact on our personal brand. Rather than wallow in self-pity and wonder about what-ifs, sometimes we do best by simply accepting and moving on. By letting go of the disappointments, we allow our self-confidence to strengthen and our personal brand to develop and shine.

THE FARRAKHAN FAKE-OUT

During my four years at WNEV-TV Channel 7 in Boston, my biggest bump in the road to awesomeness could be described in three words: Minister Louis Farrakhan.

In 1988, eighteen months after returning to Boston a married woman and being hired by Channel 7 as a production assistant, I applied for and was named a freelance contributing reporter for the station's weekend public affairs program, *Urban Update.* One day, I was assigned the enviable task of joining news reporter Miles O'Brien out to the University of Massachusetts Amherst to cover Minister Louis Farrakhan's speech. I was ecstatic. I was to assist Miles in gathering MOS (man on the street) interviews but could also use footage for *Urban Update.* Miles and I got along very well, so I was happy he was the reporter assigned to the story. We drove separate cars out to Amherst. It was freezing cold and I was a bit uncomfortable, but the excitement of the experience overshadowed that discomfort.

After the reporting duties ended, Miles thanked me for my hard work, climbed inside the Channel 7 news truck, and headed home. I jumped in the other cameraman's car. We set out on the two-hour drive back to Boston. After about an hour, the cameraman and I both realized we hadn't eaten all night. We pulled over to a small hole-in-the-wall all-night diner. After about ten minutes and to our amazement, in walked Minister Farrakhan and his Fruit of Islam security team. I couldn't believe it! My mind began to race. *What should I do? What were the chances of this happening? Could it be fate? Was this my time to grab an exclusive with the elusive? Could this be my ticket to the network news scene?*

My cameraman suggested I call Miles on his cell. I did. Miles was great. He calmly suggested I simply ask Minister Farrakhan for an interview and go from there. The station would be supportive, so I didn't have to worry about that. Miles had my back. That's all I needed to hear.

Squirming in my chair, mind swirling and unable to eat, I was a nervous wreck. I gathered my tail, hid my nerves, and confidently strolled up to The Nation of Islam leader. The protective shield quickly formed.

I addressed the member of the Fruit of Islam who appeared to be my biggest roadblock.

"Hello, sir. My name is Denise and I'm with Channel 7 in Boston. Is it possible to have just a few minutes of Minister Farrakhan's time to do a short interview with me? My cameraman is over there."

The security detail took a moment to size me up and then excused himself while he checked.

I watched him whisper to the minister. A smiled crossed the minister's face. Okay, that's a good sign, I thought. The security detail came back to me. "Minister Farrakhan said to give him some time to eat. He's tired and just wants a few minutes to rest. And then he will let you know."

"Okay. Thank you. I'll wait over there. Thank you."

I walked back over to the table and updated my cameraman. We both agreed to wait.

We waited. And waited. And waited.

After about thirty minutes, I walked back over and repeated my request. I was told to just wait a few more minutes.

We waited. And waited. And waited.

After another hour passed, we called and woke Miles. He agreed. We'd been played. My cameraman and I left. Nearly two hours of nothing. I wasn't getting an exclusive with this elusive.

I was still in the early stages of building my career and establishing my brand and this interview would have gone a long way toward achieving that goal. Perhaps it was that bright neon-lit ambition visible from across the restaurant that sealed my unfortunate fate. Perhaps the minister wouldn't have been one of the most sought-after interviews of that era if he gave in to just any twentysomething hoping to use his name to make one for herself. I decided that, if nothing else, being faked out by the Farrakhan would one day become one of the greatest stories I'd ever tell.

> **MDK BRAND TIP #7: LEARN FROM YOUR MISTAKES**
>
> Everything happens for a reason. Even though a particular experience caused by your poor judgment is painful and threatens your brand, it could turn out to be a valuable lesson you might never have learned otherwise. Apologize for the mistake, shake it off, and vow to not be so gullible again so the misstep is never repeated and your brand can thrive.

MY BRAND ON THE OLYMPIC STAGE

"This is one of those days when I'm glad I'm not you."

Those brutally honest and piercing words were spoken by my Reebok PR manager while we were at the Olympic Games in Sydney, Australia, in September of 2000. I was about to sit in front of the international press firing squad to explain the inexplicable actions of French track and field sprinter and Reebok-sponsored athlete Marie-José Pérec. In just a few days, Marie was due to compete in one of the most highly anticipated events of the Games.

One of the worst days of my career began earlier that morning as I was walking from my Reebok temporary housing to the Reebok office near the Olympic Village. I was the director of global PR for Reebok and was managing the PR program for our presence at the Games. As I was entering our temporary office facility, my cell phone began to blow up with calls from Reebok PR team members. Since I was seconds away from the office, I decided to wait to find out what the fuss was about. When I arrived at the office, anxiously pacing was the PR rep for Reebok France, Priscilla. She looked sick.

"Denise, Marie left."

"Uh, okay. When is she coming back?"

"No. I mean she left. She's gone. I took her to the airport this morning. She flew back to Paris."

I felt sick.

Priscilla then recounted the story told to her by Marie just a couple of hours earlier. It was a story that could have had James Patterson envisioning his next best seller.

According to Marie's story, intruders pushed their way inside her hotel room the night before, threatening to harm her if she didn't leave the country before her competition. I hung on Priscilla's every word.

Marie called Priscilla and pleaded for a ride to the airport. Priscilla was unsuccessful in calming Marie down and convincing her to stay.

The Reebok office phones began ringing off the hook. It wasn't even 9:00 a.m. Controversy travels fast. One of the callers was the director of the Olympics Media Center. He wanted to talk to me immediately. He'd clearly heard about the issue, which was now spiraling into a crisis. Before talking to him, I needed to wrap my head around what was unfolding and map out a game plan. Not now, I said to my team.

I expressed my confusion to Priscilla. While I was at dinner the night before, Marie called me. I knew she was upset. She told me that she believed the entire city and country wanted her out of the Olympics so Cathy Freeman, Australia's beloved track and field star, could win the gold. Marie told me she felt threatened and was scared. I talked to her for about twenty minutes, believing I'd convinced her that she was fine, no one was trying to hurt her, and all she needed was a good night's sleep. I expressed my confidence in Marie that she would win her sprint and capture the gold medal. At the end of our conversation, she seemed okay. I told her I would see her after her competition.

Instead of running her race, Marie ran away. She fled the country, leaving an unbelievable international mess for Reebok—for me—to clean up. It was a mess that threatened the credibility of both the Reebok brand and my own.

The Media Center director and I connected later that morning. Reporters were hounding him and he wasn't about to go down in flames not of his making. The international press corps was out for blood and it was my arm that needed to be extended.

After calling and conferring with my boss back at Reebok HQ, the decision was made. Like it or not, I was to be the main course for the press feeding frenzy. Within a couple of hours, I was sitting center stage at the Media Center in front of a throng of reporters from around the world. For what felt like an eternity, I endured countless, pointed questions. Over and over again, I repeated Marie's story as told to me and was unequivocal in my defense of her and her decision to flee the country in fear of her life.

First, my arm. Now, my neck.

I later read in the newspapers that Marie's story, which I assertively affirmed, was a fabrication. An untruth. A fib. It was reported that the so-called hotel room attack never happened. Some asserted that Sydney's overwhelmingly positive media coverage of its favorite daughter was too much for Marie and she simply bailed. My head was spinning. I put Reebok and my neck—my personal brand—on the line without ever checking the details of the story. I never called the hotel to ask whether there was an incident the previous night. In fact, other than Priscilla, I never asked anyone for any details. I unwisely accepted at face value a secondhand tale. It was a painful experience for my developing brand. I learned a valuable lesson and apologized to my Reebok boss, who thankfully forgave my gullibility. Never again.

***

> ## MDK BRAND TIP #8: TAKE RESPONSIBILITY, EVEN WHEN IT SUCKS
>
> Taking a hit for the team is painful but is the right thing to do when a mistake is made. Although your personal brand may be damaged because of the mistake, how you handle that mistake—taking ultimate responsibility for it and having your team's back—can make your brand stronger, whether or not that's your primary goal.

A BRAND HIT FOR THE TEAM

In March of 2013, I found myself wide awake in a professional nightmare. Nearly two years earlier, I was recruited by Boston Scientific and was its senior vice president of corporate affairs and communications. I was in San Francisco to attend the American College of Cardiology (ACC) conference, an annual gathering of the 49,000-member non-profit dedicated to improving cardiovascular health. My nightmare began unfolding with a 7:00 a.m. phone call from my director of public relations.

My director told me that one of his PR managers had mistakenly authorized the electronic distribution of an embargoed press release three hours before it should have gone out. The manager failed to account for the West Coast time zone change when she prescheduled the release to be sent via Business Wire. Boston Scientific is based on the East Coast.

The Boston Scientific press release announced the results of highly anticipated medical device research. The explosive issue my team was suddenly facing was that the results were supposed to first be announced live on stage at the ACC Conference by the principal investigator. He'd dedicated years of his professional life to this research, and announcing the results to thousands of his medical colleagues during this critical conference was most likely the exciting culmination of his work.

All ACC press releases were embargoed until the research results were presented live during the conference. The distribution of a press release prior to the live presentation of the results violated the embargo. And the punishment for violating an embargo was firm and swift. Hard as my PR director tried, explaining the innocent mistake of one of his managers due to the time zone change, ACC didn't budge. The press release being distributed three hours before the presentation violated the ACC embargo. As a result, the Boston Scientific presentation by the principal investigator was canceled! It was a nightmare. As head of the function, I accepted that the buck stopped with me. And I needed to be the one to take the hit.

We were in crisis. I immediately informed Boston Scientific executives. They were incensed. I understood. I then scheduled an emergency call with the key players so we could put a crisis plan in place. Although the damage was done and the punishment was proving to be painful, the episode wasn't over.

Near the end of the day, I was standing with a group of Boston Scientific colleagues in the San Francisco conference center when I saw the principal investigator walking with a group of other doctors. When he was alone, I excused myself from my group and did what needed to be done. I approached him and introduced myself as the head of the Boston Scientific team responsible for violating the press release embargo, which led to the ACC canceling his highly anticipated presentation. I expressed my sincere and deep apology for inadvertently causing this devastating chain of events. He could not have been more accepting of my apology. As painful as that interaction was, I knew it was necessary if I had any hope of restoring my team's reputation and my personal brand.

> MDK BRAND TIP #9:
> EMBRACE CHANGE
>
> At some point in your career, you may find
> yourself caught up in an unwelcomed reor-
> ganization that impacts your role. You can
> either begrudgingly accept the change as
> a challenge or excitedly embrace it as an
> opportunity. Embracing the change as an
> opportunity will most likely propel your
> brand and promote your awesomeness in
> ways you never expected.

KNOW WHEN TO JUST SAY YES

The call from Reebok's head of human resources was completely
unexpected. It was November 1999 and I was the senior director of
corporate communications and marketing programs at The Rockport
Company. The Reebok HR executive called to tell me that Paul Fireman
was becoming increasingly frustrated by the company's falling market
share and decreasing revenue. He was planning to once again assume
the role of president, in addition to chairman and CEO. Reebok's stock
was tanking, hovering around $8.00 a share. As such, Paul was in the
process of convening a small but key group of leaders to help him reju-
venate the brand. I was selected to be one of those leaders.

Although I was flattered, I respectfully declined the offer. I could
practically hear the HR executive's muffled laughter when he politely
pointed out that this wasn't a question or up for discussion. It was a
mandate. Paul had ordered me back to Reebok, Rockport's parent
company. Although I was disappointed at having to leave Rockport
after just sixteen months, part of me was excited to help Paul return
the Reebok mother ship back to its glory days of the 1980s and 1990s.

Excitement soon turned to doubts and fear. Could I live up to Paul's high expectations? I was determined to do just that, even if it meant working 24/7. And that's exactly how the next 365 days felt. It was the hardest I'd ever worked.

The year 2000 wasn't only a new millennium, it was a defining year for Reebok. Under Paul's leadership, Reebok ended the year as the top stock performer among the S&P 500. The following excerpt appeared in *Forbes* in January 2001:

> After suffering through diminished profits in the previous two years, the $2.9 billion (revenue) company saw its stock price more than triple, to $27.34, by the end of December. Reebok has yet to report fourth-quarter results, but in the first three quarters of last year the company earned $1.30 per share versus 45 cents per share during the same period in 1999.

The reward for topping the S&P 500 was a swanky invitation to the floor of the New York Stock Exchange. I was among the few people Paul handpicked to accompany him. It was a fantastic experience and one that began to transform and strengthen my brand.

***

MDK BRAND TIP #10: WELCOME SHORT-TERM PAIN FOR LONG-TERM GAIN

There may be times in your career when the best decision you make is to focus on someone else. In these cases, recognize that thinking about your future isn't the priority. However, in the end, whether you realize it or not, doing so will strengthen your personal brand.

THE ACQUISITION HEARD AROUND THE (SPORTS) WORLD

In the late spring of 2005, Paul Fireman, chairman and CEO of Reebok, called me to his office and disclosed his plan to sell Reebok to adidas. Paul outlined his expectation of me. I was to partner with the head of adidas communications to oversee and manage the creation and execution of the external and internal communications strategy.

A lot needed to happen before we could publicly announce the planned acquisition, and even more work was ahead before the deal could close. It was an incredible responsibility, not only because of my respect for Paul but because I recognized that billions of dollars and thousands of employees were involved.

That day marked the beginning of twelve- to fourteen-hour work-days, nearly seven days a week, for several months. Like many others assigned to the acquisition project, I had never worked so hard and under so much pressure in my entire life.

We set August 3 as the announcement date, and every member of the acquisition announcement team was focused on making sure our assignments were locked and loaded in time.

On Wednesday, August 3, 2005, at 1:30 a.m. EST, we distributed the announcement to the worldwide press, an internal letter and Paul Fireman's recorded voicemail message to employees around the world, detailing adidas's planned acquisition of Reebok.

For the next several days, the communications team was in full-steam mode, continuing to execute our comprehensive plan. We mailed thousands of letters, managed countless press interviews, monitored blogs, spoke to numerous investors and analysts, and assured employees that transparency was a top priority.

Five days after the announcement, Paul and I flew to New York to join Herbert Hainer, the president and CEO of adidas, for an intense day of meetings with press, analysts, and the commissioners of the NFL, NBA, and NHL. It would be the first time I would meet Herbert.

The meetings in New York with Herbert and Paul went very well. I only spoke briefly with Herbert and other adidas executives. Now wasn't the time to think about my career or my future. My focus was on Paul and making sure he was okay and nothing went wrong as we continued executing the communications plan.

On January 31, 2006, less than six months after the announcement, adidas's acquisition of Reebok closed. Later that same day, we announced that Paul Fireman was stepping down as chairman and CEO of Reebok and would leave the company, effective immediately. Paul declined all press interviews that day, and asked me to do them. It was a very emotional day for him and a critical moment for my personal brand. I'd been at Reebok for fifteen years. My career, my brand, grew up here. *What do I do? Where do I go from here?* I decided to stay for two years after the adidas acquisition. It was a decision that enabled me to continue to grow and develop as a corporate leader and individual brand.

***

MDK BRAND TIP #11: ACCEPT THE DAUNTING DARE

Taking on a challenge from your boss that could make or break your relationship and credibility is definitely risky. But is not accepting it a safe bet? Would you rather spend a few moments crying over a forgettable failure, or spend the rest of your career kicking yourself for not even trying? By at least trying, you'll feel empowered and your personal brand will benefit, whether or not your effort is successful. Go for it!

THE PRESIDENTIAL DARE

It was the early morning of September 23, 1995. I was in Washington, DC for the Congressional Black Caucus festivities when my hotel phone rang.

"Hello," I groggily answered.

"Hi, Denise, it's Leslie. Were you asleep?"

Leslie was a Reebok human resources executive. After a serendipitous encounter with her while I was the director of communications at Boys & Girls Clubs of Boston four years earlier, she recommended me to Reebok's head of communications. Five interviews and several weeks later, I was hired to fill the entry-level role of media relations specialist. After two promotions, I was now the manager of corporate communications.

"Hi, Leslie. What time is it?"

"It's about 7:30. Wake up, get dressed, and come meet Joyce and me at a political breakfast with Senator Carol Moseley Braun. It starts at 8:30, but we'll save a seat for you. Hurry up and get here." Joyce was a Reebok Foundation executive.

"Okay. I'll be there soon."

After getting the address from Leslie, I took a shower, put on a dress and jacket, and rushed down to the hotel's cab line. I made it to the Reebok-sponsored breakfast by 8:45.

As promised, Leslie and Joyce were saving a seat at a table inside the intimate gathering of about two hundred guests.

Senator Braun, a democrat from Illinois, was the country's first African American female senator. I was honored to be at this historic event with Leslie and Joyce. I was proud to be in the company of such strong and confident African American women. It was my first caucus and President Bill Clinton was the featured guest at this gathering of about ten thousand of the nation's "Who's Who" in African American government, business, and civic institutions.

As Senator Braun was standing at the podium delivering her moving speech, Leslie whispered to me that she and Joyce would like a photo with the senator.

"Can you make that happen?" she asked.

"Yes, of course," I confidently answered, even though I had never before managed a request of this magnitude.

My heart was pounding. I was an executive-wannabe, desperate for that big break. If I didn't come through in the next ten minutes, that dream could derail before breakfast was over.

I had no camera and no photographer. I didn't know anyone there except Leslie and Joyce. As I quickly surveyed the room, I took note of an attentive gentleman standing at the base of the stairs leading to the stage. He must be the senator's aide. Check.

I then noticed a photographer. Check. And the company I was working for was the breakfast's title sponsor. That had to help somehow. Check.

As soon as the senator finished her remarks, I jumped up from my seat and headed straight to the man I assumed was waiting for her. I overheard him telling a throng of supporters and admirers that the senator was running late for her next commitment and had to leave.

I pushed my way forward. His nametag confirmed he worked for Senator Braun.

"Hello, my name is Denise Kaigler and I'm with Reebok, the sponsor of the breakfast."

"Hi Denise," he replied.

"I realize the senator is very busy, but I'm here with two Reebok executives and I'd like to arrange for a photo with Senator Braun before she leaves."

FORTY DOLLARS AND A BRAND

As his mind was most likely sifting through all the possible ways he could deny my request, I respectfully reiterated my position.

"I'm sorry, but since we are the sponsor of this breakfast, I would really like to make this photo happen. Please."

"Unfortunately, we didn't bring a photographer with us," the staffer replied.

"Who's the photographer over there taking the pictures?" I asked.

"I don't know, but he's not with us," he said.

From the corner of my eye, I could see Leslie and Joyce anxiously awaiting the results of my negotiations. I also could see the senator trying her best to make her way off the stage through her legion of admirers. I was proving to be a distraction to her staff bouncer.

"I'll be right back," I said to the staffer.

I walked over to the photographer and introduced myself as being with Reebok. With the Reebok banner positioned as a backdrop in the room, he was already aware of our title sponsorship.

The photographer gave me his card, asked for mine, and told me he'd gladly take the photo and send it to me by the end of the day.

We rushed over to the stage. I grabbed Leslie and Joyce and respectfully requested the staffer ask Senator Braun to join us. The photograph of Senator Braun, Joyce, and Leslie was taken. Check!

Leslie and Joyce were beside themselves over that photo. They kept congratulating me on rising to the challenge and figuring it out when I had no resources.

After hanging out together for a few more minutes, Leslie, Joyce, and I made plans to meet in the hotel lobby later that evening for the black-tie Black Congressional Caucus dinner. I then headed back to the hotel, where I worked for a few hours.

Later that evening and outfitted in a long black-and-white gown, I made my way through the cocktail reception at the Congressional Black Caucus gala, my first trip to this magnificent ball. After about an hour or so of sipping cocktails and making small talk with folks a lot smarter, more connected, and more accomplished than I was, I made my way inside the ballroom where hundreds of beautifully set tables awaited their corporate sponsors and political guests. I found one of three Reebok tables and took a seat alongside my colleagues. I sat silently, taking it all in, realizing the historic moment I was part of. *Wow. Was this really happening?*

A few minutes later, Kate, my Reebok boss who was also in DC for the gala, sat across from me. Shortly thereafter, Joyce and Leslie joined. With our table full, we all began talking, laughing, and sharing our stories of the day.

"Kate, you would have been very proud of Denise today," Leslie blurted. "She was amazing."

"Oh, really. What did she do?" asked my boss.

I watched intently and quietly.

"She went with us to the Congressional Black Caucus breakfast and we gave her a huge challenge," said Joyce.

"We wanted a picture with Senator Braun," added Leslie. "And even though we didn't have a photographer, Denise figured it out and got the photo. It was incredible. Again, great job!" said Leslie.

I smiled and remained silent.

"So, Denise," Kate started. I could tell from her tone that I wasn't going to like where this was heading.

"Yes, Kate?" I carefully asked.

"I would love a picture with President Clinton. Can you make that happen? Can you handle that challenge?"

She laughed as if she assumed that I would fall flat on my face with a seemingly impossible request. It felt almost like a dare. Daring me to do something is like catnip. I couldn't resist the opportunity to prove to my boss that no challenge was beyond my resourceful capability. At least, that's the story I was telling myself.

"Yes, I can handle that. You ready?"

"Ready for what?"

"To get your picture with the president. Come on. Let's go."

I quickly stood and turned to leave. Joyce and Leslie provided some reassuring words of encouragement as I set out on what would either be a boom or bust.

"Kate, just stay close behind me. Keep up. If I lose you, that will screw up everything."

Like at the breakfast, I had no photographer. But this was worse. This wasn't a senator. It was the president of the United States! And there were tons of Secret Service agents around. Not only was Reebok not the primary sponsor, I was in a room with thousands of other guests who probably wanted the same frame-worthy photo.

I told myself to not freak out. First things first. I needed a photographer. Instinctively, I surveyed the massive ballroom and spotted a handsome photographer wearing a Congressional Black Caucus credential around his neck. Reebok was one of several sponsors so I wasn't sure if playing the sponsor card would work, but I had nothing to lose.

I confidently walked up to the photographer.

"Hi, my name is Denise and I work for Reebok. We're one of the dinner sponsors. Are you working for the CBC?"

The kind photographer proudly answered in the affirmative.

"Great. I have a huge request. I need a photograph with my boss, right here behind me, and President Clinton. Here's my card. Can I hire you to follow me and take the photo when I motion to you? And then you send me the photograph. Will you do that?"

The look on his face was worth a thousand words. He looked down at my card. Then back up at me.

"Okay, Denise. You want me to keep an eye on you and your boss while you make your way through this huge crowd and get close enough to the president to take a picture?"

"Yes, exactly."

"I don't think you're going to get that close."

"Let me worry about that. Just don't take your eyes off of me, okay?"

"And you don't worry about me," the photographer replied. "If you get close enough, I'll take the picture."

With those words, I grabbed Kate by the arm and reminded her to stay on my heels. No matter what. We then set out to make possible the impossible.

I pushed my way through the huge crowds gathered to get a glimpse of President Clinton, who was shaking hands and offering small talk to the $1,000-per-plate dinner guests. When I got a little closer, I noticed my second challenge. A rope was separating the president from the guests. How was I going to deal with that?

Can't worry about it, I told myself. I just needed to get closer. I pushed all the way to the front of the crowd. President Clinton was just a few feet away and headed in my direction. I turned to Kate with a wide grin on my face. *Almost there*, I thought.

At that moment, a Secret Service agent appeared out of nowhere and stopped me in my tracks.

"Sorry, lady. You can't be here. You need to go back."

"But I'm trying to get a picture with the president."

"I understand. But you need to go on the other side."

"What other side?"

The agent lifted his arm and pointed.

"Way over there? That's on the other side of the ballroom!" I screeched.

"Yes, it is," he said with not an ounce of compassion.

I turned to Kate and explained the obstacle that had just been thrown in our path.

"Come on. Let's go," I said.

Once again, I pushed my way through hundreds of black-tie guests, not caring how many toes I crushed in the process. We finally arrived at the front of the line. I could see President Clinton. He was within a stone's throw. I turned to Kate, ready to declare victory.

But when I turned back toward the president, he abruptly stopped, turned around, and walked in the other direction.

"Oh, no!" I screamed. "He's leaving!"

President Clinton must have heard my painful squeal. At that moment, he turned around and our eyes met. I pounced on the opportunity. I leaned over the rope and between two Secret Service agents, lifted my hand and motioned my index finger in the gesture to *please come here*. And to my astonishment, he did!

President Clinton walked toward me and leaned in. I grabbed his arm, pulled him in, and said in his ear, "President Clinton, I work for Reebok and I'm here with my boss. She wants me to get a picture of her with you. Can you please take a picture with her? Please. This is my boss!"

I reached behind and pulled Kate forward. The president looked toward Kate and began extending his hand. It all happened in a matter of seconds. I scanned the crowd in a desperate search for my photographer. There he was! Just as he promised. I motioned to him and mouthed the words, "Take the picture! Take the picture!"

Then, before I could say, 'What the heck,' some biddy behind me grabbed the president's hand and proceeded to shake it. A few seconds later, I heard Kate say, "Hello, Mr. President. It's a pleasure to meet you. Thank you," as she shook his arm hard enough to yank it off its joint.

I wasn't ready to claim victory just yet. Not until I confirmed with the photographer that the money shot was inside that camera. Kate was giddy. I'd never seen her so drunk with excitement. I cautioned her to wait until we got the two thumbs-up. I walked up to the photographer.

"Holy cow! How did you do that?" he said. "You grabbed the president's arm! I can't believe the Secret Service agents didn't tackle you. Holy cow!"

Okay. Calm down, dude.

"Did you get the shot?" I asked.

"Yes, I got it. Two great shots. I'll send you the pictures and my bill. But seeing that was worth it. Wow. Nice job. I can't believe you made that happen."

With that, I skipped back to the table, with an ear-to-ear grin across my face.

"Did you do it?" an anxious and curious Leslie asked.

Before I opened my mouth, an excited Kate answered. "Yes, Denise did it! I met the president, shook his hand, and we got the picture. She did it!"

Two weeks later, the photos arrived. There was one shot of me whispering in the president's ear, asking him to take the picture with my boss, and a second shot of me standing between Kate and President Clinton and wildly mouthing to the photographer to take the shot. It's hard to imagine one twenty-four-hour period that could have been more beneficial to my personal brand than this day. It was an unexpected opportunity that I embraced and maximized to the fullest.

Capturing the Commander: Denise with President Bill Clinton, Congressional Black Caucus Gala, Washington, DC

***

> **MDK BRAND TIP #12: BUILD UP YOUR BRAND BANK**
>
> Try not to let fear or second-guessing diminish your confidence and prevent you from taking advantage of a spectacular brand awareness opportunity. Ignorance may not be bliss, but it's real. Don't let that deflate you or make you doubt your bold decision. And if that bold decision gets you in trouble, hope that your personal brand has banked enough support from the big boss. If it hasn't, start building that bank right now!

I SURVIVED CBS'S *SURVIVOR* (WELL, SORT OF...)

It was May of 2001. I was among the Reebok employees in Los Angeles attending the live post-finale special for the second season of CBS's smash hit show, *Survivor*. As a major sponsor of the show, Reebok received several coveted tickets to watch Bryant Gumbel host the reunion of *Survivor: The Australian Outback* competitors. The previous year, I was fortunate to have worked closely with the *Survivor* team on a public relations program, which included a media tour with *Survivor* Season 1 winner Richard Hatch.

My Reebok colleagues and I arrived at CBS Studios in LA hours before the show kicked off. Not long after being ushered inside and directed to our seats, the CBS production team fanned out to instruct the audience members of live show protocol. During the walk-around, one of the crew members came over to my section and asked if anyone wanted to ask a question during the live broadcast. With too little thought, I raised my hand. After the crew member approved my question about a contestant's controversial killing of a wild boar during one episode, he gave me clear instructions on what to do and when to do it. As I watched my lifeline walk away, the reality of what I'd just volunteered to do hit me hard. The television viewing audience for

FORTY DOLLARS AND A BRAND

the *Survivor* reunion special was anticipated to be somewhere north of twenty million. The nerves, fear, and second-guessing took over: *I can't do this. Millions of people will see me make a fool of myself. I will look like a boar caught in headlights. I'll freeze and not be able to ask the question. Is it too late to change my mind?*

The simple answer was, yes, it was too late. I was a terrified mess. Lights. Camera. Action. We are live.

I was so worried about asking my question that I couldn't enjoy what was happening in front of me. I kept practicing my question over and over again in my mind. It was time. I was given the signal to go to the microphone stand.

I stood up and somehow managed to walk about two feet without tripping and falling. After waiting about five minutes for my turn, Bryant Gumbel cued me. Before asking my question, I decided to take advantage of the global platform and give my employer a plug.

"On behalf of Reebok, congratulations, Tina." Tina Wesson was the forty-year-old mother of two who had just been named the Sole Survivor and $1,000,000 winner of Season 2. I then proceeded to ask a question concerning the blood that the contestants smeared under their eyes in the wild boar episode.

When I arrived back in the Reebok office a couple of days later, I learned that CBS execs were looking to wring my neck. My split-second decision to promote Reebok during my fifteen seconds in front of twenty-eight million people infuriated CBS and, most importantly, its other corporate sponsors. Evidently, my innocent Reebok mention was considered free advertising. I assured my bosses that no one on the CBS crew asked me to identify my company affiliation and I wasn't instructed to withhold any company mention from the worldwide audience. I was only asked about my question. In an effort to limit the damage to my brand, I expressed the appropriate level of repent and was very grateful to receive a forgiving nod from the Reebok brand president, who seemed quite delighted with the free global exposure.

> MDK BRAND TIP #13: PROJECT POISE
> AND CONFIDENCE
>
> When you project poise and confidence
> and are respectfully assertive in trying to
> achieve a particular goal, anything is pos-
> sible. Doors could open. Ceilings could
> shatter. Walls could crumble. Therefore,
> act confident. Behave as if you belong.
> Don't hesitate or second-guess yourself.
> No matter how unlikely, believe you can.
> And you will.

MY HARRY BELAFONTE MOMENT

For many years, Reebok sponsored and hosted the annual Reebok Human Rights Awards ceremony where four young activists were awarded for their heroic actions on behalf of victims of human rights abuses around the world. Working on and then leading the public relations team for the ceremony was among the most rewarding experiences of my career. One of the highlights of the ceremony was the star power. Year after year, A-list celebrities accepted Reebok's request to serve as unpaid award presenters.

Among my responsibilities, I organized and hosted the pre-ceremony press conferences and organized the post-ceremony interviews that paired the celebrity with his or her human rights honoree. It was a PR person's dream assignment. At times, I was also asked to help identify possible celebrity presenters. One year as we neared the big day, the director of the Reebok Human Rights team came to my cubicle and fretted that we hadn't yet secured enough celebrity presenters. It was time to move to Plan B. She had a secondary list of celebrities who hadn't been asked to be a presenter. The problem was that the ceremony was just a couple of weeks away. Any celebrity would quickly realize he or she was part of the second tier.

The director asked me to look over the list and see if there was anyone I knew and could call. Not surprising, none of the names were stored in my little black book. No hotline to their hotline. No smoke signal secret messaging plan. Nada. With no magic wand to wave, I put my budding brand to the test. I picked out a name on the list, lifted my telephone receiver, and dialed the number. It was after 6:00 p.m., so I figured—I hoped—he would either answer the phone himself, or someone who had one foot out the door would.

"Hello, Mr. Belafonte's office," said the young woman on the other end.

"Hi, it's Denise. Is Harry there?" No last name and no company reference meant that, of course, Harry Belafonte knew who I was! Where's my Emmy?

"Denise, you said?"

"Yes, it's Denise from Reebok. Is he there?"

"Umm…" Her mind was clearly deciding her next move. I waited for what felt like an eternity.

"Hold on, please."

I looked at the director, whose eyes were as wide as headlights. And then, the sexiest voice I had ever heard sang in my ear.

"Hello?"

"Hello, Harry?"

I couldn't believe I called him Harry! In addition to being completely shocked that he actually got on the phone, I found myself caught up in the character of confidence I was feigning.

"Yes."

"Hello, Mr. Belafonte," I said, coming to my senses and showing the utmost respect for this true legend.

"My name is Denise Kaigler and I'm with Reebok. I'm calling to see if you received our invitation to serve as a presenter during the Reebok Human Rights Awards ceremony. We'd love it if you could come and help honor the young human rights activists."

I then gave Mr. Belafonte the specific date and location of the event. Did it matter that I was visualizing the crossing of my toes and fingers during this white-lie tale between two cities, Boston and New York?

"Thank you, Denise. I'm so sorry. I would love to come but I'm leaving for South Africa tomorrow morning."

Masking my disappointment, I thanked Mr. Belafonte for his time and wished him a safe trip. Even though we didn't secure his star-power participation, that brief experience buoyed my brand among the human rights team and strengthened my self-confidence. From then on, I truly believed I could accomplish anything.

***

> ### MDK BRAND TIP #14: JUST DO IT. YOU'LL REGRET IT IF YOU DON'T
>
> Though hard, it's important that you confront your fears and accept a bold assignment. If you don't, you may unknowingly miss out on a fantastic opportunity that could catapult your brand and your career. Take a chance. In the end, most people regret what they didn't do, not what they did.

THE REEBOK BRAND'S COOL FACTOR

It's hard to do justice to my level of fear during the period when I served as Reebok's director of public relations and talent relations. Reebok chairman and CEO Paul Fireman and the marketing team were on fire—signing celebrities to promote the company's new signature collection, Rbk. After the deals were signed, my job was to help activate those celebrity partnerships through announcement events and PR. And they came—celebrities with either a signature Rbk shoe, such as Pharrell Williams (Ice Cream by Rbk), 50 Cent (G Unit by Rbk), Allen Iverson (The Answer by Rbk), and Scarlett Johansson (Scarlett "Hearts" by Rbk)—or those designing for an existing athlete endorser. This was the case for Diane von Fürstenberg, who designed an Rbk apparel collection for tennis phenom Venus Williams. For each of these Rbk signature deals, I worked with my team to conceptualize, plan, and execute creative PR launch events.

Reebok had never before ventured down this path, and Paul hand-picked me to help lead the marketing communications charge. I loved every scary minute of it.

The scariest of moments occurred in 2003 when we were preparing to launch Reebok's signature JAY-Z shoe, S. Carter by Rbk. JAY-Z agreed to do two launch events in Europe. At about 4:00 p.m. the day before JAY-Z was to head to Europe, I received a call from the Interscope Records executive who helped spearhead the Reebok deal with JAY-Z. The executive had a sudden and unavoidable conflict and was unable to accompany Jay to Europe and asked me to go in his place. What? This wasn't happening. With my heart pounding, my mind was on overload: *I have never met JAY-Z. He doesn't know me and I certainly don't know him.* The executive went on to tell me that at 9:00 p.m. the next night, I would be on a private jet with JAY-Z to London to manage the press launch of one of the industry's most exciting and surprising partnerships. I would then accompany JAY-Z to Paris for the second launch event.

Okay. This *really* wasn't happening.

The next night, my Reebok photographer and I, along with JAY-Z and members of his team, boarded a private jet and headed to London. I didn't say much to JAY-Z on the flight. I was certain he wouldn't be interested in making happy talk with this corporate stand-in. We arrived in London about ten minutes before the press conference was to begin. The venue was packed. After I checked in with the onsite crew, I ran to the restroom, splashed water on my face and arm pits, brushed my teeth, quickly slipped on a black suit, and took a deep breath. JAY-Z was fantastic. He couldn't have been more enthusiastic about leading Reebok through its unchartered era of urban cool. The next night, we headed to Paris, where JAY-Z's endorsement of Rbk was equally enthusiastic and compelling. I couldn't believe I was here, at this place in my life and career. What were the odds? And what if I hadn't accepted the assignment? Turning down this opportunity out of utter fear would have caused irreparable damage to my personal brand inside my professional world and, perhaps worse, I would have never proven to myself that I could do it. I have no doubt that the unknown would have haunted me for years.

***

> ## MDK BRAND TIP #15: GO HIGH WHEN THEY GO LOW
>
> When someone blatantly disrespects you, take a deep breath and think through your response. Sometimes that response is simply to bite your lip and restrain yourself, even if you'd feel better throwing out a few choice words and waving your favorite finger in their direction. Your thoughtful reaction to someone's thoughtless action will embolden you and protect the long-term health of your personal brand.

AWESOMENESS INTERRUPTED

When I received a call from The Rockport Company's internal recruiter about joining the company as its senior director of corporate communications and marketing programs, I was both excited and torn. I had recently been promoted to director of public relations at Reebok, something I'd worked very hard to achieve. I used that fact as an excuse to not seriously consider the recruiter's outreach. But the truth was that I was scared to my professional core. I hadn't yet had a role where I was the sole and clear leader of a team, and only two levels removed from the company president. Could I cut it? As an African American woman and the only person of color on that team, would anyone listen to me? Would I be taken seriously? But the recruiter and the hiring manager, Rockport's head of global marketing, reiterated their confidence in my ability to take the communications and marketing programs team to the next level and make significant contributions.

I scheduled a meeting with Reebok's Paul Fireman and made him aware of Rockport's offer. Paul expressed his support of my accepting the offer but made it clear that he was still my boss since Reebok owned Rockport. Those words were hidden behind a warm and supportive smile, but I definitely got the message.

It was 1998 when I packed up my Reebok shoes and headed about forty-five miles west, to the more casual lane of The Rockport Company based in Marlborough, Massachusetts. Angel Martinez, who played a critical role in making Reebok a household name in the US in the 1980s, was now Rockport's charismatic president and CEO. Angel seemed to enjoy the opportunity to transform this sleepy brand into a more culturally relevant player. And I would be a key contributor in that exciting quest.

That same year, Rockport signed transgender icon RuPaul as its spokesperson. As head of marketing programs, I was responsible for planning an event to introduce Rockport and our RuPaul sponsorship to LA's celebrity scene. My charge: Throw the bash of all bashes. I flew to LA and met Carl Bendix, the owner of Ambrosia, the posh Malibu event marketing firm that manages such high-profile events as the Governor's Ball, the post-Oscars dinner gala. Carl and I clicked immediately and would build on your friendship through the years. We began mapping out a plan to host a cocktail reception that would feature a Rockport shoe display that celebrities would peruse before selecting their complimentary pair to take home. I presented the plan to Rockport executives. With two thumbs up, it was game on.

On September 8, Rockport arrived, Hollywood-style. It was unlike anything the brand had ever done. The event was attended by a couple of hundred people, each snagging a free pair of Rockport shoes and enjoying a reflexology foot massage. In addition to Rockport spokesperson RuPaul, celebrity attendance included Fran Drescher and Jane Seymour. For a while, Jane and I kept in touch and I got to know her family. She even invited me to the set of *Dr. Quinn: Medicine Woman* during a couple of my LA visits. The Rockport party was a win for the company, Angel, and my team. It was a solid example of being disruptive in a crowded marketplace and one that I will always remember fondly.

One Rockport experience wasn't so fondly remembered, and would go down as one of the most disrespectful moments I suffered through in my entire career. In my role, I was often in Rockport's New York showroom hosting reporters and organizing press events. On one particular afternoon in 1999, a few months after Angel returned to Reebok, I was getting ready for a media event to showcase Rockport's upcoming line. I was standing in the showroom talking to a Rockport executive when a group of white businessmen entered. The businessmen graciously approached the Rockport executive, who was also white, and greeted him with handshakes. As I stood next to the executive, the inquisitive stares from the businessmen at me were awkward, to say the least. Sensing his visitors' discomfort, the executive decided to introduce me. The problem was, he didn't introduce me as Rockport's senior director of corporate communications and marketing programs. Instead and inexplicably, the executive said of me, an African American member of Rockport's senior leadership team, "Oh, yes, this is Denise Kaigler. She carries my bags."

The shocked and surprised reaction from the visitors woke me from my jaw-dropping daze. I glanced at the mortified men. Then I stared down the executive. I waited for about fifteen seconds, believing in my heart of pissed-off hearts that he would apologize for his callous joke. He did not.

Through clenched teeth, I tried to put an end to the madness by telling everyone that the executive was wrong and I was in no way charged with carrying his bags. I introduced myself, turned, and walked away, leaving a trail of smoke in my path. For a moment, I contemplated going back and giving the executive an X-rated piece of my mind. But I knew that doing so would cause irreparable damage to my brand. I chose to leave it alone. Although that decision still weighs on me, I have no doubt that had I gone lower when the executive went low, my brand would not have flown as high as it did in the months and years to follow.

***

> ## MDK BRAND TIP #16: DON'T LET ANYONE DISRUPT YOUR BRAND JOURNEY
>
> One of the harshest realities of personal branding is to understand that your brand may not be embraced or even recognized by everyone. It may take a cringe-worthy moment to make the point, but don't force your brand on someone disinclined to accept it. Having your brand rejected isn't fatal, and it can only disrupt your journey toward awesomeness if you let it. So don't.

THE WILL SMITH SNUB

Will Smith is undoubtedly an exceptionally talented entertainer who has established a multi-dimensional brand worth multi-millions of dollars. The former Prince of Bel-Air has won numerous awards, including the 2002 BET Award for Best Actor in a Lead Role for his portrayal of Muhammad Ali in the self-titled 2001 film, *Ali*.

Thanks to the Interscope Records executive who was also serving as a Reebok marketing consultant, I had a front-row seat with him during the BET ceremony at LA's Kodak Theatre on June 25. When we entered the theatre to take our seats, we approached a group of celebrities milling about the front row near their seats. I walked a step behind the executive as he approached the celebrities and greeted them, one by one, with a handshake or brotherly hug for the men and a cheek or air kiss for the women. He was a gentleman and introduced me to everyone, including Will and Jada Pinkett Smith. They were both cordial in greeting me with a warm handshake. *Nice*, I thought.

The executive and I took our seats directly in front of center stage. He was to my right and the actor known as Leon was to my left. On the other side of the executive was the actor Chris Tucker. At the end of our row sat the Smiths.

Pinch me, I was on Cloud Nine. That cloud would soon burst, letting loose a fierce thunder-and-lightning storm, unexpectedly striking my personal brand.

As Will Smith was making his way to the stage to accept his Lead Actor award, the crowd was on its feet and enthusiastically applauding. The executive and I were standing and clapping as well. I watched Smith walk down the front row toward me—kissing, hugging, high-fiving his celebrity buddies along the way. I was torn about whether I would reach out to Smith to shake his hand or simply continue smiling and clapping. Smith was getting closer. The live television camera was following closely behind, peering over Smith's shoulder, forever capturing the moments of elation.

Here he comes. What should I do? Do I extend my hand? If I don't, would that be considered rude? I don't know him, but I just met him, so does that count? Make a decision. Oh no, here he is!

I took the leap, extending my hand to offer a congratulatory shake of Smith's. And then the unthinkable, unimaginable, and inconceivable happened. The scene unfolded in slow motion. There was an eerie silence inside my head. Smith brushed past me as if I was a speck of dust on a lamp, a dead fly on the floor, an ant scurrying up a hill. There wasn't even an acknowledgment of the outreached hand seen by more than seven million viewers!

Not so nice.

In total shock and unbelievably embarrassed, I dropped my hand and turned to watch Smith bear hug my executive escort. It was a deliberate snub, on the scale of nothing I'd ever experienced. The message this mega-star sent to me was clear: My brand was nowhere near the level of his brand, and acknowledging my existence by grasping my hand, regardless of how genuine the gesture, was never going to happen. My brand was more than bruised. It was carved up like a turkey on Thanksgiving.

Did this really happen? Was this like Season 9 of Dallas when Bobby Ewing wasn't really dead? Is this all a dream?

With the world now no longer rotating on its axis, I sat back down and contemplated the ways in which I would need to repair my critically injured ego. As painful as it was to relive, the first step was to acknowledge that, yes, it happened. And then to move on. This moment was not going to define me. My bruise will heal and my journey will continue.

***

> MDK BRAND TIP #17: HAVE FAITH YOUR BRAND WILL SURVIVE AND THRIVE
>
> Family comes first, and protecting that priority may temporarily weaken your personal brand as you climb the professional ladder. As long as you can look at yourself in the mirror and have no regrets about decisions made because of your family, that's what's important. It may take time, but your brand will survive, evolve and thrive.

BICOASTAL LIVING: OUR NEW NORMAL

It was early 2008. Joe and I called a family meeting. It was time to unveil the big news and hope the tornado would be short lived and the damage minimal. Dani was in the tenth grade, an emotional rollercoaster year by any definition. Joey, who was in the seventh grade, idolized his sister. Her reaction would influence his reaction, so the key was to secure her support and understanding. Okay. It was time.

"Guys, daddy and I need to tell you something," I started. The kids were sitting next to me on the family room sofa. Joe was sitting nearby at the breakfast bar in the kitchen, a safe distance from the looming tornado.

"I've been at Reebok for a very long time and have been offered a great opportunity to do something else very exciting." Dani looked eerily frozen.

"The new job is at Nintendo, the videogame company, and it's in San Francisco, California. Daddy and I talked a lot about it and we agree that it's something we should do, so I've accepted the job." Dani immediately began to wail.

"I don't want to move to California! My friends are all here!" She started sobbing hysterically.

Joey's bewilderment degenerated to sadness, then fear. Tears welled up in his eyes and streamed down his face. He looked scared, shocked, and confused.

"No, honey. We're not moving. We will keep this house and we'll also get a place near Nintendo. I'll fly back and forth between home and work. You and Joey won't have to leave your school and daddy won't have to leave his job."

With those soothing words, the faucet of tears shut down. A smile crossed Dani's face and then she said, "Okay, mommy. That's great. Wow, Nintendo, that's so cool."

"Wow, that is cool. Do we get free games?" asked my excited little man, clearly receiving the all-clear-to-support-mommy-and-be-happy nod from his big sister.

I spent the next several weeks closing down a seventeen-year career at Reebok, updating friends and family, finding a place in San Francisco, and setting up our bicoastal lives. I'd always wanted to live in California, dating back to college. The distance from the East Coast where I grew up made my mother uneasy, so I never pushed it. This was my chance to fulfill a lifelong dream.

The first several months at Nintendo were filled with excitement and fear. How was I going to be an involved mother working three thousand miles from my kids? A doting wife who saw her husband two weekends a month? A caring friend whose relationships were distant and impersonal? I worked primarily out of Nintendo's Redwood City, California, office and spent one week each month working out of the New York office where several of my staff members worked. I traveled monthly to Nintendo's US headquarters in Redmond, Washington, where most of its US executive team members were based, and spent time in Kyoto, Japan—where Nintendo's global headquarters is located.

The excitement of Nintendo was addictive. From taking center stage in New York's Times Square during a launch event to being invited by a famed videogame designer to join him on stage at the videogame industry's annual E3 conference, I spent my time at Nintendo enjoying a fantastic and exhilarating ride.

That ride started coming to an end in the fall of 2009. The constant travel was taking its toll. I was a nomad. Whenever I was in San Francisco, I knew I had to leave at any moment. And when I was home in Boston, I knew I had to leave at any moment. I had no real base. No place to firmly lay my head for any real length of time. Dani was in her junior year of high school and the dreaded college application process was fast approaching. It was time for me to focus on my daughter and help her through a process that would impact the rest of her life.

I left Nintendo, returned home, and immersed myself in planning Dani's future. Although I was unsure about the next phase of my career and the future of my personal brand, I knew that my family came first and I would be fine.

> **MDK BRAND TIP #18: LIFT AS YOU RISE**
>
> The late Prince recognized the power of his brand, and he leveraged that power to give back to an organization that gave so much to him. As you're building your brand, remember those who remembered and helped you. If a Prince can lift as he rose, we all can!

THE PRINCE AND PAISLEY PARK

The feeling I was experiencing was surreal. As a public relations manager at Reebok, I couldn't believe I was at Paisley Park, the famed home of the late mega-musician, Prince. There aren't too many homes that have their own brand. The White House and the Playboy Mansion come to mind. I was working very closely with the National Newspaper Publishers Association (NNPA) and its newspaper members around the country. During its national conference in Minneapolis, the NNPA asked to host an intimate opening reception at Paisley Park. The request was granted. I later heard that Prince granted the request out of gratitude and thanks. The NNPA had been unwavering in its support of Prince from the very beginning of his career, well before he became a one-name brand. The black newspapers had given Prince much-needed exposure and visibility within its influential and broad network. And it appears he never forgot it.

Prince was traveling and not present during the memorable reception. Apparently, he left specific instructions to his staff. We were taken on a tour, had a fantastic dinner, and ended the evening with a private and intimate one-woman concert by Mavis Staples of the Staples Sisters. The experience was beyond amazing. Me, a black girl from Washington, DC, sitting in Prince's palace being entertained by one of the most iconic voices in the music industry. Unbelievable.

> ## MDK BRAND TIP #19: PREPARE YOUR NEXT CHAPTER
>
> Being prepared with your next chapter before you need it can protect your brand. If you suddenly find yourself caught up in a downsizing, layoff, or job elimination, you will be able to transition quickly and evolve your personal brand in a way that is viewed as strategic and smooth. If you are prepared with your next chapter, you will be able to turn the unexpected into a fabulous opportunity.

PLANNING MY NEXT CHAPTER

At the 2013 Massachusetts Conference for Women in Boston, a realization hit me like a spray of ice cold water. I was at a session when the speaker urged the thousands of women in attendance to plan their next chapter. With those words, I had an 'uh-oh' moment. I didn't have my next chapter planned. At the time, I was the senior vice president of corporate affairs and communications at Boston Scientific. I had been traveling quite a bit while balancing the demands of motherhood. My insane work and family schedule left little time for life planning. But it was nuts to assume that what was working well today would be perfect the next day, month, or year. And that was the point. Life happens. Be prepared for it. At that moment, I was not.

Moments change.

Within a few weeks, I began crafting my next chapter. What was my post–Boston Scientific plan? I decided that I would no longer just dream of starting a business. I would do it. Although I loved communications and public relations, my passion for personal branding—a passion that began in college—now included a passion for corporate branding. My love for and experience in corporate branding began during my Reebok tenure and was now on full throttle at Boston Scientific. A year earlier, my team and I led the comprehensive global rebranding of Boston Scientific, which included my writing the company's brand declaration, "Advancing science for life." Riding that high, I began testing the brand management waters. It started with volunteering my time facilitating personal branding workshops for Boston Scientific's black employee resource group, Bridge. Soon thereafter, I approached the president of the NAACP Boston branch and asked if I could volunteer my time to facilitate personal branding workshops for his organization. He loved the idea and suggested I work with the NAACP's Young Professionals Network. Perfect. Later that summer, I spent several Saturday afternoons facilitating personal branding workshops for NAACP YPN members. The experience was exhilarating and helped me start putting together my next chapter.

In late 2014, I received a call from a former Reebok colleague who was working for United Way of Massachusetts Bay and Merrimack Valley. She told me the organization was preparing to analyze the impact of its nonprofit brand and asked if I was available to facilitate a branding session during a full day leadership retreat. I was thrilled and immediately accepted. I took the morning off from Boston Scientific and facilitated a ninety-minute branding workshop for seventy-five members of United Way's leadership team. As I was leaving the retreat, I was informed that numerous members of the leadership team had very positive feedback about my session. The feedback was so positive that I was asked if I had ever given thought to starting my own branding company. While becoming an entrepreneur was a dream of mine, the reality was that quitting my senior-level, regular-paycheck job and leaving corporate was scary. But following a second well-received branding workshop for United Way in March, 2015, I began wondering if this was the catalyst that would lead to my next chapter, a business owner. In fact, it was.

In July of 2015, just three weeks after my Boston Scientific job was eliminated as part of a reorganization, I founded MDK Brand Management, LLC. Preparing my next chapter before I needed it allowed me to transition quickly and smoothly from corporate to entrepreneurship. It was the best decision I could have ever made.

> MDK BRAND TIP #20: LIVE YOUR AWESOMENESS!
>
> Believe in who you are and the purpose you serve during this life. Embrace the brand you have or have confidence in your ability to define the brand you want. Believe that you are awesome, that you can overcome challenges and defy the odds. Enjoy all that life—your career—has to offer. It won't always be easy. You may make a wrong decision, a bad move, a regrettable error. But that's not the end of the story. You will smile again. The sun will rise again. And you will live your awesomeness.

YOU ARE AWESOME

If you don't believe it, who will? If you don't feel deep down to the very core of your human essence that you are worthy, that you are beautiful, that you are valued, how will anyone else? Awesomeness is not defined by material possessions, bank accounts, physical appearance, or any single element. It's the impact we have on others, the commitments we make and keep, and the value we place on ourselves. An investment in you—whether real or intangible, made by you or someone else—could be the difference between existing and living. But it is up to you to make the most of it. It will, at times, be challenging, but use that investment to overcome the challenges, defy the odds, and live your awesomeness.

When I was younger, I felt intense disappointment when someone told me they would do something, and then never followed through. I never quite understood why someone would do that. In my mind, you either did what you said you would do, or you told the person the reasons you couldn't do it—before it was to be done. What was so hard about that? I felt that admitting and explaining the need to change a plan mitigated whatever disappointment was on the horizon. As an adult, I didn't want others to associate their disappointment with anything I did or did not do. That fueled my desire, my need, to follow through on my commitments and to meet or exceed expectations. I ran when others walked. I arrived early and stayed late. I focused on the details, no matter how seemingly small. I accompanied my bosses to events just to make sure they had whatever onsite support they needed. I made tough decisions and accepted difficult tasks. I laughed and enjoyed the ride and worked to create an environment that encouraged my employees to do the same.

Through the years, I have enthusiastically embraced and nurtured my brand of getting sh*t done and delivering results. It has enabled me to live a blessed life and build a wonderful career. I have traveled around the world and met amazing people, including the late boxing great Muhammad Ali, President Jimmy Carter, South African social rights activist Bishop Desmond Tutu, civil rights pioneer Rosa Parks, actor and humanitarian Robert Redford, actors Danny Glover and Alfre Woodard, and many others. I have enjoyed incredible experiences, including walking the Great Wall of China, touring an underground command center in Ho Chi Minh City, Vietnam, and eating dinner overlooking the Panama Canal. However, it wasn't all smooth sailing. There were several times in my career when I should have made a better decision, acted in a different way, done something else or nothing at all. I'm not perfect. I'm not infallible. However, despite sailing through some rough waters, including my 30-year marriage ending in divorce in early 2017, I continue to feel great about the many blessings in my life. I have stayed true to my values, remained comforted by my faith, embraced my sense of purpose, and reaffirmed the importance I place on my family and friends. I know with absolute certainty that I did not get here alone. I owe so much to so many.

Now that you have completed Part I, I hope you were able to learn from the twenty tips and stories from the trenches of my career as you set out to overcome challenges and defy the odds. Moving on to Part II, I encourage you to complete your Personal Brand Workbook, which includes Six Steps to discovering and living your awesomeness. Enjoy!

PART II
YOUR PERSONAL BRAND WORKBOOK
SIX STEPS TO DISCOVERING AND LIVING YOUR AWESOMENESS

DISCOVERING AND LIVING YOUR AWESOMENESS

"Whatever you can do, or dream you can, begin it. Boldness has genius, power and magic in it."

—Johann Wolfgang von Goethe

Building and marketing a defined personal brand during your journey to awesomeness will not be easy. You may encounter challenges and face overwhelming odds. Navigating this brand labyrinth takes careful planning and consistent execution. The following six steps outline the primary ways to build and market your personal brand and discover your awesomeness. These steps include activities and worksheets for you to complete.

Following the six steps does not guarantee you will achieve all of your goals, but if you are willing to make the investment, completing the activities and worksheets will help strengthen the confidence you have in your ability to discover and live your awesomeness. Each step is followed by a related story that I hope you will find motivating.

BE WILLING

STEP 1: BE WILLING

The first step to reaching a goal or achieving something you want very badly is to mentally accept that it may be a challenge. That means having the willingness to make the effort and the investment. As you work to define and develop your desired brand, be willing to take on whatever challenges lie ahead. As the saying goes, "nothing worth having is ever easy."

THE ACTIVITY

Check the appropriate boxes. Then write two or three additional vows or promises you are willing to make as you work toward living your awesomeness:

☐ 1. I will make a commitment to do everything I can to fulfill my potential.

☐ 2. I will work hard to keep a positive attitude, even when life throws obstacles in my way.

☐ 3. I will stay away from negative influences focused on knocking me down and keeping me from achieving my goals.

☐ 4. I will be supportive of my friends and family so they can also achieve their goals.

☐ 5. I will take the time to invest in my future as a positive role model and leader.

Other:

_____

_____

_____

_____

_____

Signature: _____

Date: _____

THE WILL TO LOVE

Meeting a parent for the first time after eighteen years of neglect is an incredibly emotional experience. The realization that my father had made a deliberate decision to ignore me during my entire childhood was painful and incensing. I was fourteen when my mother inexplicably arranged a phone call between her former suitor and his two daughters, Debbie and me. It was the first time my father and I had ever spoken. Despite hundreds of miles separating us, my father somehow managed to reach through the fiber optics and touch every ounce of my soul. Unfortunately, it would be another four years before he would touch my soul again.

When I turned eighteen, I called my mother and asked for her help in finding my father. She gave me my paternal grandfather's phone number. Ma assumed that since my father no longer had any legal obligation to me, he would be more likely to accept and embrace me as his daughter.

Periodically through the years, I had been in touch with my grandfather. And although I'd even met him once, he hadn't before wanted to get in the middle of the drama between his son and my mother. I hoped that this time, my grandfather would share the belief that my legal adulthood removed the feared handcuffs from his son's wrists. Apparently, he did.

After getting my father's phone number from my grandfather, I took a deep breath and dialed.

"Hello," a male voice answered.

"Hello, is this Michael?"

"Yes, who is this?"

"It's Denise."

"Denise, who?"

"Denise, your daughter."

With those words, there was a lengthy and palpable silence. Two hours and lots of laughter and tears later, my father and I made plans for him to arrange my flight to Cincinnati, Ohio, to meet in person.

During that Cincinnati visit, my father and I caught up on the past eighteen years. We definitely had moments of yelling and blaming. Our time together was fun, stressful, frustrating, enlightening, and, most of all, perfect. I was an impressionable, directionless teenager who had just found her black knight. Sure, that black knight rode off into the sunset without me shortly after I was born, and I made sure he was acutely aware of how that decision impacted my life.

For the first several months of knowing my father, I only addressed him as Michael. He was patient and understanding until the day I called him Michael in front of his friends. He soon gave me an ultimatum: Call him father, daddy, pa, whatever. But if I called him Michael again, he would ignore me. Having a relationship with my father was something I'd dreamed of my entire life. I couldn't lose him now. From that moment on, I embraced him as my daddy.

It's interesting how life works. I was eighteen when my father and I met for the first time. He was eighteen when he and my mother conceived me. We were both teenagers when fate stepped in. I wasn't going to let his irresponsible decision eighteen years ago seal our forever. We were both willing to make the investment in our relationship and in our future. And thank God we did. Today, nearly four decades later, my daddy is my best friend. I love him deeply.

In addition to having the will to build the relationship with my father, I was willing to accept the challenges of my personal brand and to make the effort and investment in evolving my brand to help me achieve my goals and live my awesomeness.

My Brand Then...

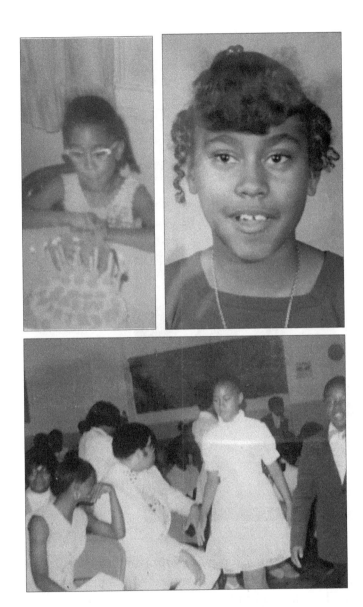

Denise is a shy introvert, with no self-confidence,
no self-esteem and no identity

My Brand Now...

Denise with Chace Crawford at Nintendo event in NYC

Denise with Alfre Woodard and Danny Glover at Reebok event

Denise speaking at United Way Women's Leadership Breakfast in Boston

Denise is a former television news reporter-turned-corporate executive, and now entrepreneur, author, and adjunct professor who has a defined and confident brand.

DEFINE YOUR DESIRED BRAND

STEP 2: DEFINE YOUR DESIRED BRAND

Don't leave the way you are viewed or judged up to someone else's vision, definition, or interpretation. Take control of your career, your future, and your life by defining how you want to be regarded today and remembered tomorrow. You have the power to influence opinions and affect attitudes. Start exercising that power today.

THE ACTIVITY

1. Decide what you want others to think or believe about you. What kind of impact do you want to make?

    Such as:

    - You get the job done, no matter the obstacle.
    - You are all about results. Effort is nice, but not enough.
    - You are the most organized person on the team.
    - Your intelligence and resourcefulness are vital.

    Fill in your responses below:

    - _____

    - _____

    - _____

    - _____

Fill in your name and desired brand description below:

I, _____ ,

want to be viewed as someone who:

_____

_____

_____

_____

My desired brand is:

☐ Realistic

☐ Authentic

☐ Sustainable

I want my brand to help me achieve my:

☐ Personal goals

☐ Professional goals

☐ Both

A HOLE-IN-ONE FOR MY BRAND

In 1994, I was handed a terrific opportunity that would help establish the brand I wanted to project in the corporate world: Confident, dependable, and hardworking. Reebok had signed on to serve as a major sponsor of the Black Enterprise Golf and Tennis Challenge being held at the PGA National Resort & Spa in Palm Beach Gardens, Florida.

Reebok was running on all cylinders and, as a result, employees were working endless hours and juggling countless balls. I was a public relations manager when I received a call from one of the company's vice presidents asking to meet with me about the BE Challenge. I was intrigued. He informed me that Reebok was committed to ensuring a strong presence at the event but had no one internally to organize all the sponsorship details and manage our onsite presence. I was tapped to lead that effort. I happily accepted (not that I had a choice!).

For the next several weeks, I was head-down in intense event planning and worked directly with the Graves family, which owns and manages Black Enterprise magazine. The Reebok team and PR agency Circulation Experti headed to Florida a few days before the September event. It was grueling and stressful but, in the end, we hit a hole-in-one. Reebok's presence was so strong that we received a standing ovation during the Welcome Dinner. Thanks to the opportunity to organize and manage Reebok's sponsorship of the Black Enterprise Golf and Tennis Challenge, my wanting to project a brand known for being confident, dependable, and hardworking was realistic, authentic, and sustainable.

STEP 3

SURVEY OTHERS

STEP 3: SURVEY OTHERS

Although others are aware of your existence, what do they think of your personal brand? What are your positive and negative attributes? To build your brand, you must have clarity on your strengths and weaknesses, challenges and opportunities, talents and limitations. What are the differences between what you see in yourself and what others see in you? It's time to find out.

THE ACTIVITY

YOUR PERSONAL BRAND SURVEY

Your personal brand survey should consist of no less than ten questions designed to elicit useful information for your brand development. After you write the questions and finalize the survey, distribute the survey to ten or fifteen of your contacts. To ensure the most honest feedback possible, consider having someone else e-mail the survey on your behalf. Or you can also choose to distribute the survey via an online tool such as SurveyMonkey. Be sure to include both professional and personal contacts (e.g., work, school, community). I've included a few sample questions to help get you started. (To keep it simple, I use 'her' in the questions but you should insert 'him' if appropriate.)

1. What five words come to mind when you think of [insert your name]'s personal brand? Please explain the reason for choosing each word.

2. What do you believe is her primary strength? What actions demonstrate that strength?

3. What do you believe is her primary weakness? What actions demonstrate that weakness?

4. If you could give [insert your name] one piece of advice to enhance her personal brand, what would that be?

5. Do you believe [insert your name] is or has the potential to be a leader, or is she best suited to be a follower? Why?

6. When you encounter [insert your name], how would you describe her presence? Consider the following: Does she command the room? Project confidence? Lead or contribute to a stimulating conversation? Is she well put together? Does she use correct grammar?

7. Do you have confidence that [insert your name]'s personal brand can help her achieve her professional or personal goals? If so, why? If not, why not?

To help you stay organized, write your survey recipient names and date below and then check off the names as the survey responses are received:

Your Name: _____

Survey Distribution Date: _____

Survey Recipient Names	Response Received
1. _____	☐
2. _____	☐
3. _____	☐
4. _____	☐

5. _____ ☐

6. _____ ☐

7. _____ ☐

8. _____ ☐

9. _____ ☐

10. _____ ☐

11. _____ ☐

12. _____ ☐

13. _____ ☐

14. _____ ☐

15. _____ ☐

SURVEYING MY BRAND

Throughout my career, my performance has been reviewed by my peers, employees, and superiors. That feeling in the pit of my stomach twice each year as I sat in front of my boss was enough to make me want to burn rubber and hurl in the closest toilet. The reviews weren't just of my work performance, but a peek inside of what people thought of me personally. Was I too hard on my employees, too impatient when pushing to exceed results, or too unforgiving when mistakes were made? Was I too aggressive or too mild, too outspoken or too muted? Or was I simply not doing a good job or meeting expectations? Whatever the answers, knowing them was more important than whether I agreed with them. When you are aware of what people think of you, it gives you control. It might be difficult, but try to learn from feedback. I did and it has made me a better and stronger person, both professionally and personally.

WRITE YOUR ELEVATOR PITCH

STEP 4: WRITE YOUR ELEVATOR PITCH

If you had just one minute to make a strong impact and leave a memorable impression, what would you say? How would you say it? Don't wait to figure this out at the moment you need it. It could happen at an elevator, a social event, a networking activity, or a work-related conference. Chances are, one day you'll need an elevator pitch. Planning for it now will remove any fear and uncertainty and will help you project a strong and confident brand.

Do you have a pitch? If not, let's get started:

TEN TIPS FOR WRITING YOUR ELEVATOR PITCH

Write and memorize your primary pitch. Understand that one pitch may not be appropriate for all audiences. Your primary pitch should include the main points of your background and showcase your brand. Depending on the scenario—audience, objective, and the amount of time you have to make a strong impression—be prepared to mentally edit that primary pitch.

1. **Research your audience** — It helps to understand what your audience will be interested in knowing about you. This will help you tailor your pitch so you're not eliciting the dreaded eye-roll or mind-roam. You won't always have this opportunity, but when you do, plan ahead.

2. **Know your objective** — What's your end goal? Do you want a job, a promotion, an internship, a board seat, a college admission? Your end goal will help you prioritize the content of your pitch.

3. **Start strong; what's your headline?** — Your initial goal is to make an immediate impression. Start your pitch with a memorable, catchy, unique or impressive statement about yourself, your career, or your background.

4. **Connect your professional endeavor with your "Why," if appropriate** — Why do you do what you do (or strive to do)? Why are you inspired to travel down your professional path? If your "Why" is not appropriate for or relevant to a particular audience, feel free to leave it out of your pitch.

5. **Showcase your authenticity** — Confidently highlight the credentials, experience and skills that are relevant to your audience and can help you achieve your objective. These credentials can include your experience and education as well as any publications you've authored or events you've organized.

6. **Keep it conversational** — Don't sound like you're simply rehearsing a memorized pitch. Practice makes smooth and seamless. During your pitch, take a couple of brief pauses to provide opportunities for your audience to ask questions or interject comments.

7. **Make a connection** — Try to find something you have in common with your audience that you can reference. That will establish a comfortable tone. If that doesn't exist, reference current events or overall relevant observations about your surroundings or environment.

8. **Tell your story, don't oversell yourself** — We all like a good story but we don't like being cornered in a sales pitch or listening to someone go on and on about their greatness. Be compelling without overselling. Test out your pitch by reading it to someone you trust and who will give you honest feedback.

9. **Set stage to continue the conversation** — It's generally considered uncouth to ask for what you want during an initial encounter. Suggest or request a follow-up meeting, perhaps over coffee or lunch.

10. **Offer your personal business card** — Create and selectively offer a personal business card with your personal email address and cell number. This will ensure you're reachable should you leave your current employer.

DENISE'S ELEVATOR PITCH

Hello. I'm Denise Kaigler. After 25 years of working for global brands, including Reebok, adidas Group, Nintendo and Boston Scientific, I now help clients discover and live their awesomeness. In 2015, I made the leap to entrepreneurship and founded MDK Brand Management, LLC. I was inspired to focus on brand management because I used to be a shy introvert, with no self-confidence, no self-esteem and no identity. I put myself through college and worked my way into and up through a competitive corporate environment, learning lots of life-lessons and developing my brand along the way. I am now using my personal background and challenges to help clients develop a defined and confident brand that can help them reach their professional goals or achieve their business objectives. If you have a need to create or strengthen your personal brand or your organization's identity, may I schedule time on your calendar? Here's my card. May I have your card?

THE ACTIVITY

WRITE YOUR BRAND ELEVATOR PITCH

_____

_____

_____

_____

_____

_____

_____

_____

_____

_____

_____

_____

_____

_____

_____

_____

_____

_____

MY NEAR-MISS PITCH

My first critical opportunity to pitch my budding personal brand took place literally outside of an elevator. It was in 1992. I had been at Reebok for about a year and was working at a junior level. It was about 6:00 p.m. and I was leaving after a tiring day.

As I stood at the elevators adjacent to several executive offices, out walked Paul Fireman, the company's chairman and CEO. I had yet to meet Paul but I certainly recognized him. Paul looked at me and asked who I was, where I worked, and for whom I worked? Momentarily paralyzed, I stood there, at the threshold of what would either be a strikeout or a grand slam. In those few seconds, I hoped against hope that I would make a memorable impression. But I faced a seemingly insurmountable obstacle: I did not have a planned response. With little time for hesitation, I reached back to my reporter training and managed to string together something decent. That experience demonstrated to me very early in my career the importance of being ready to maximize an opportune moment to leave your indelible mark.

The day in 2006 when Paul left Reebok following its sale to the adidas Group was one of the saddest days of my career. I will always fondly remember and be appreciative of Paul's leadership, support, and friendship, and for making sure I never struck out.

BRAND THROUGH MEANINGFUL ACTIONS

STEP 5: BRAND THROUGH MEANINGFUL ACTIONS

Just thinking about ways to demonstrate your desired brand isn't enough. You must take deliberate action to ensure others know who you are and what you stand for. If you want to be known as a thought leader on a particular subject matter, consider taking on volunteer projects focused on that particular area. If you want to be known as a kind and giving individual so that you might land your ideal job as the development director for a nonprofit, consider volunteering for, and perhaps leading, a fundraising campaign. If you want to be known as being organized and detail oriented, but the general feedback from your brand survey shows that you're late for meetings, disorganized, and unfocused, you've got a problem. But don't fret. Consider sending out an agenda before the meeting, having copies of the agenda at the meeting, distributing a summary following the meeting, and definitely showing up on time or a few minutes early to the meeting. How are you demonstrating your desired brand?

THE ACTIVITY

Keep track of your meaningful, brand-building actions. Examples of actions could include helping someone in need, serving as a mentor or coach, donating your time to a community center, volunteering your expertise, or taking on and leading a project at work, school or church.

What are your brand-building actions?

1. _____

2. _____

3. _____

4. _____

5. _____

6. _____

7. _____

8. _____

9. _____

10. _____

MY MEANINGFUL ACTIONS

As I was thinking about my next chapter and contemplating entrepreneurship in brand management, I volunteered my time facilitating personal and organizational branding sessions. I hosted personal branding workshops for the Boston NAACP Young Professionals Network and Boston Scientific's black employee resource group. I also led an organizational branding workshop for United Way of Massachusetts Bay and Merrimack Valley. These workshops began to establish my brand management thought leadership.

DISCOVER AND LIVE YOUR AWESOMENESS

STEP 6: LIVE YOUR AWESOMENESS!

Once you have executed actions designed to establish your desired brand, how are you living it? These are the behaviors and activities you are incorporating in your regular routine that help to maintain your brand by continuously projecting its key attributes.

Get Out There

1. Join and be active on volunteer boards or with community organizations.
2. Attend and be appropriately sociable at networking events, industry conferences, or school trips.
3. Produce and strategically distribute personal business cards (include your name, personal e-mail address, cell number, an inspirational quote, and your website URL if you have one).
4. Write and post compelling blogs, opinion pieces, and expert commentary on social networking platforms.

THE ACTIVITY

Awesomeness Log: Tracking Your Activity

How are you living your awesomeness (e.g., blogs, posts, panels, networking events)?

	Activity	Date
1.	_____	_____
2.	_____	_____
3.	_____	_____
4.	_____	_____
5.	_____	_____
6.	_____	_____
7.	_____	_____
8.	_____	_____
9.	_____	_____
10.	_____	_____

MY AWESOME ACTIVITIES

Once I laid the groundwork for establishing my reputation as a brand management thought leader, I planned and executed many activities designed to live and maintain it. These activities included sitting on panels, speaking at conferences, and writing brand-related posts. Blogs, in particular, are an effective way to demonstrate your thought leadership on a particular topic to a broad audience. This will be great visibility for you and your brand.

CONCLUSION
OUR SIMILAR DIFFERENCES

I have flown on a private jet to Europe with JAY-Z, participated in a Reebok endorsement pitch meeting in LA with Gwen Stefani, and had dinner and hosted a press conference in Boston with Scarlett Johansson. I have organized a fashion show in London with Venus Williams and Diane von Fürstenberg, spearheaded back-to-back Reebok events in Philadelphia and New York with 50 Cent and Allen Iverson, and launched Wii Sports Resort in New York with Gossip Girl's Chace Crawford. I have worked on the Reebok Human Rights Awards program with numerous celebrity presenters, including Richard Gere, Kerry Washington, Cameron Diaz, Blair Underwood, Susan Sarandon, Don Cheadle, Wanda Sykes, Sting, Vernon Jordan, and George Stephanopoulos. My extensive global business travel has spanned numerous countries around the world, including Australia, China, Costa Rica, England, France, Greece, India, Indonesia, Ireland, Japan, Korea, Mexico, Monaco, Panama, Spain, Thailand, the United Arab Emirates, and Vietnam. I have attended nearly every major sporting event on the planet, including the Super Bowl, World Cup, Wimbledon, French Open, US Open, NBA All-Star Game, MLB World Series, and the Olympics.

On the outside, I was a confident and secure corporate leader. But on the inside, I remained a shy, introverted DC girl fighting to be valued and needing to be appreciated. I was terrified of failing and being shoved back inside my invisible box tucked away inside my nothingness world.

While our experiences may seem worlds apart, the emotional, mental, and physical investment needed to fulfill our individual potential is more closely aligned than it would seem. During my journey, I made the conscious decision to accept and embrace who I am—flaws and all. It took time, but making this decision eventually made a world of difference in my professional and personal life. Respecting our weaknesses while leveraging our strengths is not an easy process. But it must be done.

If you haven't already done so, make the decision to define, develop, and market your desired brand. Hold your head high and move with confidence toward overcoming your challenges, defying the odds, and living your awesomeness.

AUTHOR'S ACKNOWLEDGMENTS

My heartfelt thanks and appreciation to my family, friends, mentors and supporters who stood by me, cared about me, and helped me discover and live my awesomeness.

ABOUT THE AUTHOR

Michela Denise Moore (Kaigler) was born in Huntington, West Virginia and raised in Washington, DC. A shy introvert, Denise confronted her fears and applied to the broadcast journalism program at Emerson College in Boston, MA. After financing her education through student loans, grants, scholarships, and part-time jobs, Denise earned a bachelor of arts degree in 1985, worked briefly for Boston City Council President Bruce Bolling, and began her career as a television news reporter at WLTZ-TV, the NBC affiliate in Columbus, Georgia.

Following a brief stint as a freelance journalist in Boston at WNEV-TV, the CBS affiliate, and as the director of communications for Boys & Girls Clubs of Boston, Denise joined the corporate world in 1991. During the next twenty-four years, her corporate career in communications, public relations, and brand management excelled. She held leadership roles at Reebok, adidas Group, Nintendo, and Boston Scientific. After her senior-level position at Boston Scientific was eliminated in June of 2015, Denise wasted no time in fulfilling her dream of entrepreneurship. She founded MDK Brand Management, LLC three weeks later. In October of 2015, she officially launched her company with three clients, including Boston Scientific. In addition to helping organizations define and enhance their identities, Denise is committed to helping individuals develop a defined and confident personal brand. In January of 2017, Denise took on the additional role of adjunct professor and enjoys supporting students at Lasell College in Auburndale, MA, and the University of Massachusetts Boston.

Denise is the proud mother of Danielle and Joey Kaigler.

YOUR PERSONAL BRAND JOURNAL

_____

_____

_____

_____

_____

_____

_____

_____

_____

_____

_____

_____

_____

_____

_____

_____

_____

_____

_____

_____

_____

_____

_____

_____

_____

_____

_____

_____

_____

_____

_____

_____

_____

_____

_____

_____

_____

_____

_____

_____

_____

_____

_____

_____

_____

_____

_____

_____

_____

_____

_____

_____

_____

_____

_____

_____

_____

_____